The Transformation
Of Activism

*Trans-*action Books

The Transformation
Of Activism

Edited by
AUGUST MEIER

Trans-**action** Books

Published and distributed by
Aldine Publishing Company

The essays in this book originally appeared
in *Trans*-**action** Magazine

for two from Morgan:
SHERMAN AND HAYWOOD
and three from Kent:
HENRY AND DINA
AND TOM

Contents

Preface

However diverse their attitudes and interpretations may sometimes be, social scientists are now entering a period of shared realization that the United States—both at home and abroad—has entered a crucial period of transition. Indeed, the much burdened word "crisis" has now become a commonplace among black militants, Wall Street lawyers, housewives, and even professional politicians.

For the past six years, *Trans*-action magazine has dedicated itself to the task of reporting the strains and conflicts within the American system. But the magazine has done more than this. It has pioneered in social programs for changing the society, offered the kind of analysis that has permanently restructured the terms of the "dialogue" between peoples and publics, and offered the sort of prognosis that makes for real alterations in social and political policies directly affecting our lives.

The work done in the pages of *Trans*-action has crossed

disciplinary boundaries. This represents much more than simple cross-disciplinary "team efforts." It embodies rather a recognition that the social world cannot be easily carved into neat academic disciplines. That, indeed, the study of the experience of blacks in American ghettos, or the manifold uses and abuses of agencies of law enforcement, or the sorts of overseas policies that lead to the celebration of some dictatorships and the condemnation of others, can best be examined from many viewpoints and from the vantage points of many disciplines.

This series of books clearly demonstrates the superiority of starting with real world problems and searching out practical solutions, over the zealous guardianship of professional boundaries. Indeed, it is precisely this approach that has elicited enthusiastic support from leading American social scientists for this new and dynamic series of books.

The demands upon scholarship and scientific judgment are particularly stringent, for no one has been untouched by the current situation. Each essay republished in these volumes bears the imprint of the author's attempt to communicate his own experience of the crisis. Yet, despite the sense of urgency these papers exhibit, the editors feel that many have withstood the test of time, and match in durable interest the best of available social science literature. This collection of *Trans*-action articles, then, attempts to address itself to immediate issues without violating the basic insights derived from the classical literature in the various fields of social science.

The subject matter of these books concerns social changes that have aroused the long-standing needs and present-day anxieties of us all. These changes are in organizational life styles, concepts of human ability and intelligence, changing patterns of norms and morals, the relationship of social conditions to physical and biological environments, and in the status of social science with national policy making.

This has been a decade of dissident minorities, massive shifts in norms of social conduct, population explosions and urban expansions, and vast realignments between nations of the world. The social scientists involved as editors and authors of this *Trans*-action series have gone beyond observation of these critical areas, and have entered into the vital and difficult tasks of explanation and interpretation. They have defined issues in a way making solutions possible. They have provided answers as well as asked the right questions. Thus, this series should be conceived as the first collection dedicated not to the highlighting of social problems alone, but to establishing guidelines for social solutions based on the social sciences.

THE EDITORS
Trans-action

$Introduction$

AUGUST MEIER

The term "activism," as applied to the civil-rights movement, first gained currency in the early 1960's, when it was used to contrast the activities of those who engaged in nonviolent direct action with the NAACP's "legalistic" strategies of lobbying in the legislatures and conducting litigation in the courts. Because *Trans*-action did not begin publication until late 1963, when nonviolent direct action had reached its crest, and, more significantly, because behavioral scientists did not, for the most part, begin serious study of the black protest movement until the second half of the decade, the magazine has discussed neither the origins of the direct-action movement, nor its phenomenal successes during the late 1950's and early 1960's. What *Trans*-action has done, however, is to chronicle the decline of activism—and its transformation.

The first two selections, Charlayne Hunter's description of the Poor People's Campaign in the summer of 1968,

1

and Michael Lipsky's analysis of the New York City rent strikes, are illuminating studies of the nonviolent direct-action movement in decline. As it became clear that non-violent direct action would prove no more effective an instrument than had legalism in solving the problems of the poor, activists became disillusioned and turned to other techniques.

Urban slumdwellers, disillusioned with the limitations in the nonviolent direct-action techniques, responded with the riots of 1964-1968. These were spontaneous affairs, but there were those—including some of the most militant former practitioners of nonviolent direct action—who held that organized rebellion would be necessary to effect any really significant changes in the condition of the black masses. But as the article by Terry Ann Knopf suggests, the existence of planned attempts at armed rebellion in the ghettos has been seriously overestimated, and such efforts offer little hope as a realistic strategy.

Activism—in a modified form—survived chiefly on the college campuses. Quite possibly this was because the colleges and universities comprised the sector of American society most vulnerable to attack from young activists, both white and black. William Friedland and Harry Edwards, in their article on Cornell University, describe one of the most famous of the confrontations arising out of heightened activism among black students.

During the middle 1960's, as the millenialistic expectations earlier associated with nonviolent direct action waned, many came to pin their hopes on political action—on using the Negro bloc vote as a lever for social change. Hadden, Masotti and Thiessen, in their study of the famous 1967 mayoralty elections in Cleveland and Gary, suggest, however, that there are serious limitations to what political action can accomplish. The same warning is given even more explicitly in Donald Matthews' and James Prothro's *Negroes and the New Southern Politics.* I include here my own review essay of this volume; and while I am critical of Matthews and Prothro in many particulars, I would agree with their basic contention that although politics will be an important avenue for black advancement, it will not rapidly solve all the problems facing Negroes in America.

Substantial social change occurred as a result of the activist campaigns of the early 1960's, but the basic economic problems of the black masses remained unsolved and Negroes were still scarcely represented in the economic and political power structures of the country. One result of the disillusionment and discouragement with the pace of social change was a retreat into a militant rhetoric that rejected the goal of Negro integration into American society. The selections by Joyce Ladner and David Riesman on Black Power, and by Ulf Hannerz on the concept of "Soul" illustrate this trend. Miss Ladner, while sympathetic toward the advocates of Black Power, admits that it is a term that is not well-defined, and she is unwilling to predict that it will accomplish much in the future. As Hannerz suggests in his evaluation of the significance of "Soul," one can say that these are rhetorical devices, offering immense psychological satisfaction in the face of the enormous problems that lie ahead before black men can achieve full equality in American society.

The conclusions of the contributors to *Trans*-action are fundamentally pessimistic ones. The millennium in American race relations has not come, and will not come in the near future. No one tactic, nor all of them together, provide a panacea. As the selections collectively imply, the heyday of the nonviolent direct-action activism of the early 1960's, with all its dramatic and soul-stirring victories, was but the end of the beginning in the struggle for a racially just society in America.

Kent State University   *August Meier*
Kent, Ohio

On the Case
in Resurrection City

CHARLAYNE HUNTER

Resurrection City—where the poor had hoped to become visible and effective—is dead. And despite the contention of many people, both black and white, that it should never have been born, R.C. was, as its City Fathers had been quick to point out, a moment in history that may yet have a telling effect on the future of this country. For although Resurrection City was never really a city, per se, it functioned as a city, with all the elements of conflict that arise when public issues and private troubles come together.

The public issues were clear and could be articulated—at least in a general way—by most of the people who lived there. Handbills had helped residents formulate their statement of purpose. "What will the Poor People's Campaign do in Washington?" read one handbill. "We will build powerful nonviolent demonstrations on the issues of jobs, income, welfare, health, housing, human rights. These massive demonstrations will be aimed at government centers of power and they will be expanded if necessary. We must make the government face up to poverty and racism." If such a statement was not specific enough, residents—who in all probability found it difficult to always know just what the leaders had in mind (as did the leaders themselves)—would simply fend off the question with a statement like, "*We* know what the demands are." If pressed further, they would glare accusingly at the questioner, as if to further confirm his ignorance. (This technique of bluffing one's way into the offensive was initiated by the leader of the Poor People's Campaign, the Rev. Ralph Abernathy. The press was relentless in its efforts to get Mr. Abernathy to give out more specifics about his demands, but this was impossible for a long while simply because none had been formulated.)

The private troubles of those who came to live in R.C. were less clear, at least in the beginning. And as these troubles emerged—sometimes in the form of fights, rapes, thefts, and harassment—they became far more prominent than the cause or the individuals who came to fight for it. The outside world concerned itself with the disorganization and lack of leadership in the camp. And while this was certainly a valid concern, critics seemed to be missing one essential point—that the life styles of the poor vary, from individual to individual and from region to region. Long before coming to Resurrection City, leaders and followers had been conditioned by their backgrounds and the life styles they had established. That is why, for example, the first City Manager of R.C., Jesse Jackson—a 26-year-old Chicagoan and an official of the Southern Christian Leadership Conference (S.C.L.C.)—had more success with the Northern urban hustler than did Hosea Williams, the second City Manager, who came out of the South and had much more success with diffident rural blacks.

Most of the conflicts at the camp were caused by the ghetto youths whose lives in the asphalt jungles of the North led them to view Resurrection City as a camp-outing and an alfresco frolic. Surrounded by trees, grass, and open air, the Northern youths were among alien things, which (before the rain and mud) were hostile to them. The innocence of their Southern counterparts—for whom the trees, grass, open air, and mud are a way of life—was a challenge to the Northerners. With such easy, church-oriented prey, the hip cat from the North immediately went into his thing—taking advantage of the uninitiated. Southerners had the history of the movement behind them. They had produced the sit-ins, the Freedom Rides, the Bus Boycotts—the 1960's Direct Action Task Force. And yet much of the Southern mystique got beaten by the hard, hostile life style of the urban ghetto-dweller.

No one is quite sure how many people moved into Resurrection City, although there was an attempt to register people as they came in. The registration count was 6312, but the community was nothing if not mobile and there was no way to count the outflow.

The people came to the District from all sections of the country. They came in bus caravans and on trains. Some came from the South in the Mule Train (which was put into a regular train in Atlanta because the horses were giving out), some came from the nearby North in cars or on foot. They came representing the church. They came representing the community. They came representing street gangs—those that would fight and those that wouldn't. And many came representing themselves. Most came as followers. But, of necessity, a few emerged as leaders. Many came to participate in the campaign for as long as S.C.L.C. wanted them there, and then they planned to go home. Others came thinking of the North as a land of opportunity. And *they* came to stay forever.

Today, the site where Resurrection City stood is cleared. After the sun baked the mud dry, patches of growing grass were placed there, and although the land is not quite so green as it was before, it is just as it was when the architects began designing Resurrection City on paper back in April. Perhaps if they had it to do over, they would change a few things, because, by now, they would have learned about the differences in poverty—that poor people do not automatically respond positively to one another.

The design, on paper, had been impressive. Three architects (none of them Negroes), with the help of students of the Howard University School of Architecture (all of them Negroes), produced plans that called for modest A-frame structures, which could be built small enough for two and large enough for six or eight and which would house 3000 people for two to four months. The prefabricated units—25 percent of them A-frames and 75 percent of them dormitories—were to be assembled in Virginia by local white volunteers, then brought to Washington in trucks that would be unloaded next to the building sites, starting west and building eastward.

By the time the first stake for an A-frame was driven in by Mr. Abernathy, around a thousand people had already come into Washington and had been housed in coliseums and churches.

During the first week, morale and energy and activity levels were high. But one of the first indications that the paper plans might not succeed came when the New York delegation insisted upon setting up shop in the most easternward section of the site. New Yorkers, independent, fast-paced, and accustomed to protests (like rent strikes) that require organization, were going to do things their own way. Though this meant that they had to carry their own wood all the way from the front of the site to the back, they set up their structures with record-breaking speed. Where it sometimes took three men working together an hour to put up an A-frame, in the New York contingent three men produced an A-frame in 15 minutes. There was, among *everyone,* a feeling of distrust for larger communities: Provincialism had reared its head.

After a week and a half of more or less organized endeavor, there followed a long stretch of bad weather. It rained every day, and rivers of thick, brown mud stood in doorways and flowed along the walkways from one end of the camp to the other. But although the mud and rain sapped some of the energy of some of the assemblers, it seemed to inspire creativity in others—the majority, in fact, since they were eager to get their houses built so that they could move in. More people came to R.C. than left. And although many had been evacuated to churches and schools—often long distances away—the Mexican-Americans and the Indians were the only contingents that chose to stay on high ground.

When the rains did not let up, the last vestiges of formal organization at R.C. slid unceremoniously into the mud. But those who had left returned, and others joined them, and all waded through. Wood that had been lost turned up as porches for the A-frame houses—luxuries not called for in the paper plans. "It was interesting to see this mass-produced, prefab stuff developing into color and rambunctiousness," one of the planners said.

By the time most of the A-frames had been filled, what existed on the site of the planned city was a camp rather than a community, with some areas so compounded with picket fences or solid fences that no outsider could get in. Walking or wading through the camp, one saw not only simple, unadorned A-frames, but split-levels and duplexes. Some were unpainted; others were painted simply (usually with yellows and burgundy); and still others were both mildly and wildly, reverently and irreverently, decorated with slogans. One house bore on its side a verse from the Bible: "And they said one to another, behold, this dreamer cometh. Come now therefore, and let us slay him, and cast him into some pit, and we will say, some evil beast hath devoured him: and we shall see what will become of his dreams. Genesis 37. Martin Luther King, Jr., 1929-1968." Others had such slogans as "Black Power on Time," "Soul Power," "United People Power, Toledo, Ohio," "Soul City, U.S.A.," and "The Dirty Dozen," on a building I figured was a dormitory. And, of course, the inevitable "Flower Power." "I Have a Dream" stickers appeared in most places, as well as pictures of Martin Luther King—usually enshrined beside the canvas-and-wood cots inside the houses.

Just as the slogans varied widely, so did the inside appearance of the houses. While many looked like the wreck of the Hesperus, in others, by 9 A.M. when the camp was opened to visitors, beds were made, clothes were hung, floors were swept, and—in several houses—plank coffee-tables were adorned with greenery in tin-can vases.

The Coretta King Day Care Center was perhaps the most successful unit in the camp. A local church group contributed most of the materials, including books like *Alice in Wonderland, What Are You Looking At?, The Enormous Egg,* and Bennett Cerf's *Pop-Up Lyrics*. There were even toy cars and trucks, water colors, and jigsaw puzzles. And a hundred pairs of muddy boots. The children played games and sang songs such as "If You're Happy and You Know It, Clap Your Hands" and, of course, "We Shall Overcome." And they went on field trips—to the Smithsonian, the National Historical Wax Museum, and Georgetown University. Enrollment was about 75.

Altogether, Resurrection City never contained more than the average American city—the bare-bone necessities. Still, many people received more medical attention than ever before in their lives. A young mother left Marks, Miss., with a baby whose chances of survival, she had been told, were very slim. He was dying of malnutrition. After three weeks of medical care—vitamins, milk, food—he began gaining weight and life. For others, teeth were saved. Upper-respiratory infections—at one point a source of alarm to those outside the camp—were treated and curbed. And when one of the residents died while on a demonstration in the food line at the Agriculture Department, there was little doubt that it was not Resurrection City that killed him, but the lack of adequate medical attention back home. Most of the residents were also eating better. The menus were often a hodge-podge affair—sometimes consisting of beef stew, turnip greens, apple sauce, and an orange—but the food was nutritious. And you did not need food stamps to get it.

Residents of Resurrection City found it difficult to understand the outside world's reaction via the press to conditions within the camp. The stink from the toilets that filled one's nostrils whenever a breeze stirred was, as one observer put it, "the smell of poverty." Residents put it another way. "I appreciate the mud," a woman from Detroit said. "It might help get some of this disease out."

The mud of Resurrection City was seen by many as unifying, if not cleansing. Andy Young, an S.C.L.C. executive, trying to dispel rumors of disorganization in the camp, said one day: "We are a movement, not an organization. And we move when the spirit says move. Anything outside is God's business. We are incorporated by the Lord and baptized by all this rain."

While the camp was virtually leaderless from a formal, organizational standpoint (Mr. Abernathy was always off traveling with a large entourage of S.C.L.C. officials), it did not lack individual movers and doers. One day, a discussion of the mud revealed such a person. Standing attentively at a press conference on a sunny day, with an umbrella over her head, Mrs. Lila Mae Brooks of Sunflower County, Miss., said, to no one in particular, "We used to mud and us who have commodes are used to no sewers." A tall, thin, spirited woman, Mrs. Brooks talks with little or no prompting. Observing that I was interested, she went on: "We used to being sick, too. And we used to death. All my children [she has eight] born sickly. But in Sunflower County, sick folks sent from the hospital and told to come back in two months. They set up 27 rent houses—rent for $25—and they put you out when you don't pay. People got the health department over 'bout the sewers, but Mayor said they couldn't put in sewers until 1972." She is 47, and for years has worked in private homes, cotton fields, and churches. In 1964 she was fired from a job for helping Negroes register to vote. For a while, she was on the S.C.L.C. staff, teaching citizenship. When she had a sunstroke, and later a heart attack, she had to go on welfare. (She is also divorced.) For three years, she got $40-a-month child support, and finally $73. She left her children with her mother, who is 80, and sister to come to the campaign.

"People in Sunflower asked my friends was I sick 'cause they hadn't seen me. Then they saw me on TV in Washington and said I'd better head back before the first or they'd cut off my welfare check. You go out the state overnight and they cut off your welfare check. But that's OK. I had to come. When S.C.L.C. chose me from Eastland's County, he met his match. I've seen so much. I've seen 'em selling food stamps and they tell you if you don't buy, they cut off your welfare check. And that stuff they sell there don't count—milk, tobacco, and washing powder. Well, how you gonna keep clean? All the welfare people know is what *they* need. I ain't raising no more white babies for them. Ain't goin' that road no more. I drug my own children through the cotton fields, now they talkin' 'bout not lettin' us go to Congress. Well, I'll stand on Eastland's toes. People from 12 months to 12 months without work. People with no money. Where the hell the money at? I say to myself, I'll go to Washington and find out. Talking about using it to build clinics. Then they make people pay so much at the clinics they get turned away. What the people gettin' ain't enough to say grace over. I done wrote to Washington so much they don't have to ask my name."

I asked Mrs. Brooks how long she planned to say here. "I don't know, honey," she said as she put her sunglasses on. "They just might have to 'posit my body in Washington."

There were other women organizing welfare groups and working in the lunch halls, and still others, like Miss Muriel Johnson, a social worker on loan to S.C.L.C. from other organizations. This was her first movement and she was in charge of holding "sensitivity" sessions. When I asked her what a sensitivity session was, she said, "Well, you just can't take a bunch of people out and march them down Independence Avenue. All they know is that they're hungry and want something done about it. We got 150 to 200 people out a day into nonviolent demonstrations. We got to teach them to protect themselves and prepare for whatever. We have to explain situations to people. And we have to talk with them, not down to them. If they get something out of this training, they'll go home and do something."

Joining Mrs. Brooks and Miss Johnson were many other young men and women, among them college students who, like the students of the old movement (the early 1960s), believed that it was better for black boys and girls to give themselves immediately and fully to a worthwhile cause than to finish college. Many of them wore their hair natural and some wore buttons that said, "Doing it black." Young men like Leon and J.T., both S.C.L.C. organizers in the South, held no place in the movement hierarchy, but were, as the residents were fond of saying of anybody plugged in to what was going on, "on the case."

Leon and J.T. led demonstrations and boosted morale by taking part in the day-to-day problems and activities of Resurrection City. The difference between them and many of the other S.C.L.C. officials was that when R.C. residents were tired and smelly from marching eight miles to a demonstration and back, so were Leon and J.T. When residents went to bed wearing all their clothes and wrapped in blankets saturated with dampness, so did Leon and J.T. And if Leon and J.T. could still sing freedom songs the next day, then so could they. There were not, however, enough Leons and J.T.s. Many weeks had been spent building the Abernathy compound—a large frame structure surrounded by A-frames for his aides. But despite a ceremonial gesture of walking in with a suitcase and announcing that he was moving in, Mr. Abernathy never lived in R.C. Nor did his lieutenants.

One of the most effective communicators around Resurrection City was a man of a different breed from that of Leon or J.T.: Lance Watson, better (and perhaps solely) known as Sweet Willie Wine. Sweet Willie, 29, is the leader of the Memphis Invaders, the group accused of starting the riots in Memphis after the assassination of Martin Luther King. (Sweet Willie denies this.) He spent most of his time walking around the camp, wrapped in a colorful serapi, combing his heavy Afro. He condemns the Vietnam war as immoral, and of his own time in the army paratroops says, "In service I took the great white father's word. I thought it was all right to be half a man. Now it is time to question. We are questioning everything now."

When the campaign was over, most of the Invaders went home. Sweet Willie, however, is still walking the streets of Washington, occasionally plugging in to local militants, but more often holding down some corner in the black ghetto.

The Invaders bridged the gap between the diffident Southern blacks and the hustling ghetto youth from the North. Memphis, after all, is a kind of half-way place, with elements both of the Southern rural and the urban ghetto scenes. And it is perhaps because of this that they made it through to the end. The Blackstone Rangers, from Chicago, did not. Early on, they were sent home for causing trouble. Acting on the theory that if the tough guys were used as peace officers, they would be too busy keeping others out of trouble to get in trouble themselves, S.C.L.C. officials began using the Blackstone Rangers as marshals. It didn't work.

Yet most of the gangs there saw themselves more as protectors of the other black people in the camp than as participants in the campaign. The leader of St. Louis's Zulu 1200's, Clarence Guthrie, said that the Zulus did not pretend to be nonviolent, but "since this campaign concerns a lot of brothers and sisters who are working their thing, we'll use our resources to protect them."

With so many disparate elements in the camp, it only took a slight incident to cause a large group to assemble, with a great deal of fight potential. Most of the Southerners had come with an S.C.L.C. orientation, and as a result they were still singing "We Shall Overcome," including the verse "Black and white together." But few people from above the Mason-Dixon line were singing "We Shall Overcome," let alone "Black and white together." They usually ignored the whites inside the camp, who for the most part were either kids who would do all the dirty work or hippies off somewhere by themselves with their flowers. Still, any altercation outside the camp usually involved some white person. Such was the case when a fight broke out just outside the grounds. Police—mostly whites—appeared in large numbers. The Tent City Rangers, a group of older men formed as security officers, broke up the fight, but some of the boys whose adrenaline had risen headed for a white man wearing bermuda shorts and taking pictures. With dispatch, they relieved him of his camera and disappeared. The man wanted his camera back, he said, because it was expensive. But he added, "I think I understand. I come down here in my bermuda shorts taking pictures. And I guess I understand how this would make them angry."

Laurice Barksdale, a 24-year-old veteran from Atlanta, was angry, too. But he vented his frustrations in another way. From early in the morning to late in the afternoon, the sweet smell of baking bread joined the other scents in the air. In a small A-frame decorated with the motto "Unhung-up Bread," Barksdale spent every day baking bread for residents and visitors as well. The supplies had come from a white New Yorker who travels from community to community teaching people how to make bread. At R.C. he discovered Barksdale, who had learned to cook in his high school home-economics class, and set him up in business. After four years in the Marines, Barksdale had come home to Atlanta and had not been able to find a job. His mother, who worked for S.C.L.C., suggested that he go along on the Poor People's Campaign to see if he could help out. Barksdale says he's not really interested in making money. "I got a cause," he says. "And a lot of brothers and sisters around me."

The one S.C.L.C. higher-up always on the case was Hosea Williams, who early in the campaign became the City Manager. One of Hosea's major assets was the gift of rap.

One Sunday morning he was stopped by three well-dressed white men, one of whom said he was running for Congress from Florida and had come to R.C. because he felt he and his people ought to know about it. Soon after the conversation began, the man asked Hosea about his background, and if he was a Communist. Hosea was not offended by the question, but moved into it slowly. He denied being a Communist.

"What is Resurrection City all about?" Hosea asked rhetorically. "This is what you have to know. We are asking for jobs. Not welfare. Check the cat on the welfare rolls and you'll find his mother and daddy were on welfare.

"What we've got to have is a redefinition of work. As Lillian Smith indicated in her book, I think *Killers of the Dream,* what we have is a conflicting ideology in our value system. The reason I loved Dr. King was that he made $600,000 in one year and died a pauper. We have got to let scientists go to work and create jobs. I know it can be done. I was working as a research chemist for 14 years trying to rid this country of insects. I was born in Attapulgus, Ga. My father was a field hand and my mother worked in the white folks' house. I raised myself while she raised the white folks' children. And we got to get some help for the old. And we got to do something about this educational system. That's what produced the hippies. White colleges. I got more respect for the hippies than I have for the hypocrites.

"R.C. is just a place we have to sleep and get some food to fight a war—a nonviolent war. We are here for an economic bill of rights. Congress's job is to solve the problems. We are political analysts and psychiatrists and Congress is the patient."

On that Sunday morning there was a sense of movement and activity throughout the camp. This was true on any given day. Near the entrance to the camp, young boys played checkers and whist, and some were getting haircuts. Over the P.A. system in City Hall, someone was calling for attention. "Will Cornbread please report to City Hall immediately? Attention. Will Cornbread please report to City Hall immediately?" Like Leon and J.T. most people didn't know any other name for Cornbread but Cornbread. But Cornbread was a household word because he was on the case.

Also on that morning, a tall, thin, white man looking like the church pictures of Jesus took up a position behind a table near the checkers game and began making predictions—that there would be a big snow in August; that there would be a Republican President in 1972; that people of America would one day eat one another.

"Are you open to question?" someone called out. He did not respond.

The thin man continued, saying that he had prophesied the burning in Washington. He was interrupted again, by another voice from what had become a building crowd. "Tell me what the number gon' be so I can be a rich man tomorrow." An elderly Negro man with a pair of crutches next to his chair called out, to no one in particular, "Hey, where are my cigars?"

I asked the crippled man where he came from. Coy, Ala. How long had he been at R.C.? "Since they drove the first nail," he answered. "What have you been doing?" "Well, I can't do much. I've got arthritis. I usually get up about 4 A.M. and just sit here. But I tried to organize a men's Bible class like at my church back home. Not too much success, though. I had a lovely time yesterday. Seven of us went out to a church and we had services. Then we had a wonderful dinner there—fried chicken, candied potatoes, and wrinkle steaks. You know what those are, don't you?" He smiled. "If I can hop a ride, I want to go back."

Sitting behind him were two young men. One was saying, "I got to fly home to court tomorrow. Charge of marihuana. Ain't had none." The young man was from New York. It was not the kind of thing one was likely to hear from his Southern counterpart. Narcotics is the traditional way out for many of the frustrated young in the asphalt jungles of the North. Somehow, this syndrome never hit the South. A young Southern black, eager to escape the lot of his father, has one way out—the army. And many of them, once they enlist, choose to stay.

Soon another announcement came over the P.A. system asking all residents who planned to take part in the day's demonstrations to report to the front gate.

On Sundays, Resurrection City—with all its diversity— was opened up to even more diversity. Sunday was tourist day and visitors began arriving sometime after breakfast. One particular Sunday, as the residents drifted out of the front gate to a demonstration, among the tourists coming in were many well-dressed Negroes from the District on their way home from church or elsewhere (as remote as they seemed to be from things, it didn't seem likely that they would have dressed up to come to R.C.). Some whites came, too. Mainly the tourists drove by in cars, slowing down long enough to snap a picture and continue on. To the Negro visitors (who almost never wore boots to protect their shoes from the mud), most residents (who did wear boots and slept in them at night to keep warm) were cordial, sometimes condescending (something of a unique turnabout in the scheme of things)— "Yes, *do* come in and have a look around. We're right proud of what we have here." Later, at a Lou Rawls concert, which was inadvertently set up before the demonstration, but which Hosea decided to let go on, Hosea addressed the crowd and concluded with a few well-chosen words for the Negro tourists: "The police want to use those billy clubs. But they ain't gonna bother you today. Today is Uncle Tom Day, and they don't whip up on Uncle Tom heads."

Demonstrations were the one constant in R.C. Each demonstration I attended was different from another, not so much because the body of demonstrators changed as because of their usual tendency to "do what the spirit say do."

Although R.C. residents had been there before—to present demands for changes in the welfare system—my first demonstration was at the Department of Health, Education, and Welfare. The 200 demonstrators marched into the auditorium of the building and sent word that they wanted to see "Brother Cohen"—Wilbur J. Cohen, Secretary of Health, Education, and Welfare. An otherwise impressive delegation—including Assistant Secretary Ralph K. Huitt and Harold Howe II of H.E.W.'s Office of Education— was sent in, but was given short shrift. Led by Hosea, the demonstrators began to chant "We want Cohen," and Hosea turned from the second-string officials and told the crowd: "You might as well get comfortable," and before he had finished a young boy in gray trousers and a green shirt had taken off his tennis shoes, rolled up his soiled brown jacket into a headrest, and stretched out on the floor. As he closed his eyes, the crowd, led by Hosea, began singing "Woke Up This Morning With My Mind Set on Freedom." In between songs the crowd would chant "We want Cohen." An elderly lady from New Orleans, who after the march obviously had little strength left to stand and yell and chant, simply shook her head in time with whatever she happened to be hearing at the moment.

The more pressure the officials put upon Hosea to relent, the stronger the support from the crowd. Given the demonstrators' vote of confidence, he began to rap. "I never lived in a democracy until I moved to Resurrection City. But it looks like the stuff is all right."

"Sock soul, brother!" the people yelled.

"Out here," he continued, "they got the gray matter to discover a cure for cancer, but can't."

"Sock soul, brother!"

Then, to the tune of the song "Ain't Gonna Let Nobody Turn Me 'Round," Hosea led the group in singing, "Ain't Gonna Let the Lack of Health Facilities Turn Me 'Round." And at the end of the song—something like three hours after the demonstrators had demanded to see Cohen—the word spread through the auditorium: "Cohen's on the case."

Demonstrators who had spread throughout the building buttonholing anybody and everybody who looked important, demanding that they "go downstairs and get Cohen," filed back into the auditorium. And as Cohen appeared, an exultant cheer rose from the demonstrators—not for Cohen but for the point that they had won.

Before Cohen spoke, Huitt came to the microphone. He looked relieved. "I'd just like to say, before introducing the Secretary, that I haven't heard preaching and singing like that since I was a boy. Maybe that's what wrong with me." The crowd liked that and showed it. "Get on the case, brother," someone called. And as clenched black fists went into the air—a gesture that had come to stand for "Silence!" and succeeded in getting it—Cohen spoke:

"Welcome to your auditorium," he said, managing a smile. He proceeded to outline his response to the demonstrators' demands, which included changing the state-by-state system of welfare to a federally controlled one. When he had finished, he introduced a very polished, gray-haired, white matron sitting next to him as "our director of civil rights." A voice of a Negro woman in rags called out to her: "Get to work, baby."

The second demonstration I attended was at the Justice Department. Earlier in the day, as rumors grew of dissension between the Mexican-Americans and the blacks, Reiss Tiejerina, the leader of the Mexican-Americans, and Rodolfo ("Corky") Gonzales, his fiery lieutenant, appeared for a press conference to be held jointly with Hosea and the Indian leader, Hank Adams. Accompanying Tiejerina and Gonzales was a small contingent of Mexican-Americans with unmuddied feet (during the entire campaign, their group remained in the Hawthorne School, where there was not only hot food but hot showers as well), and a few Indians. Tiejerina had one major concern: regaining the land in New Mexico that, he claims, was illegally taken away from his people some 300 years ago in the Treaty of Guadalupe Hidalgo.

As the press conference broke up and the demonstrators made ready for the march, the Mexican-Americans boarded buses to take them to the Justice Department, while the preparations of the blacks consisted of a black demonstrator's shouting: "Get your feet in the street. We're marching today."

The Justice Department demonstration was officially under the direction of Corky Gonzales. His demands were that the Attorney General speak with 100 of the demonstrators, with all ethnic groups represented equally—which turned out to be 25 Mexican-Americans, 15 Indians, 20 poor whites, and 40 blacks. The Attorney General agreed to speak with only 20 of the demonstrators, and this proved totally unacceptable to Gonzales. (Tiejerina was not there at the time.)

For several days, talk of getting arrested in some demonstration had become intense. Somehow, as the hours
wore on during the Justice Department demonstration, it
was decided that this might be the place. The question
seemed to be, was it the time and was the cause broad
enough?

There were some demonstrators who came prepared for
any eventuality, regardless of the cause. As long as the
order came from S.C.L.C. Ben Ownes, 52, widely known
as Sunshine, was prepared. The crowd blocking the entrance to the Justice Department (a federal offense in itself), though led by Gonzales, was singing the S.C.L.C.
songs: To the tune of "No More Weepin', No More
Mourning," they sang, "No More Broken Treaties. . . ."
Sunshine talked about his involvement in the movement.

"In Birmingham, in 1963, friends from my church
were picketing. I went down. I didn't tote no signs, but
my boss still told me when I got back to work not to tote.
Then next time I went and toted. The third time I toted,
I didn't have a job. But I'd heap more rather work for
Dr. King for $25 a week than for $125. My house has
been threatened. My mother has been threatened. But I
registered a lot of people in Selma, Green County, Sumter
County, and many others. Sometime I be sick, but I can't
go home. I've gone too far now to turn 'round. I've been
so close to so many things. Jimmy Lee Jackson got killed.
James Reed got beat to death. Mrs. Liuzzo killed. September 15, 1963, six people were killed—two boys and four
girls. If I die for *something* I don't mind. I've been in
jail 17 or 18 times. But we really got to work in this
town."

The police, however, did not seem to be in an arresting
mood. They just stood in the street behind the demonstrators, more or less impassive. Suddenly Hosea took the
bullhorn.

"Look at those cops!" he shouted.

The crowd turned. The cops shifted uneasily. "You see what they've done," he continued, his voice rising. The crowd looked. "They don't have on their badges, so that when they take you to jail and do whatever they're gon' do to you, you won't be able to identify them." The crowd was now facing the policemen and could see that not one of them was wearing a badge. Hosea started to rap about police brutality and the sickness of America. "Just look at that!" he cried, pointing an accusing finger. And no one had to be told, this time, what they were looking for. All could see that the shiny badges had been put back in their places—on the chests of the entire cadre of policemen standing behind them. But Hosea was now into his thing. "But look," he said, again pointing. "Just to show you how sick this country is—the sickness of America and racism—*look*." The crowd was baffled. What was he talking about now? Hosea, virtually overcome with rage, now shouted, "You see how sick this country is? Otherwise how come all the white cops are lined up on one side and all the black cops lined up further down the street? Just look at it!" The division in the line was distinct. Immediately behind the demonstrators was a line of white policemen. To the extreme left of the demonstrators a solid line of black faces in uniform. Hosea rapped a good long while.

As the evening wore on, and the Attorney General did not show up and the demonstrators did not get arrested, there seemed to be some indecision among the demonstration's leaders. Hosea, at times, seemed at a loss. Corky had tired of leading the group in songs, and the demonstrators had never quite caught all the words. Corky and Hosea huddled often, only to return and lead more singing. Father James Groppi of Milwaukee showed up, received wide applause, made an impassioned speech, and joined in the singing. At one point, Hosea broke off to consult with his lawyer, and Tiejerina showed up. "What's going on?" he asked innocently. Hosea explained that the Attorney General had refused to see 100, but would see 20. "That's fine. O.K., isn't it? We send the 20?"

Hosea looked confused. "Corky is holding out for 100."

"I will talk to Corky," Tiejerina said, and good-naturedly bounced off.

The evening grew longer. The demonstrators grew tired. Few complained, but many were curious. They were not getting the usual positive vibrations from Hosea, who looked haggard and weary. Then, suddenly, as if he'd blown in on a fresh breeze, there stood Jesse Jackson, who has been described as being closer than anyone else to Dr. King in charisma and in his acceptance of nonviolence as a way of life. Jackson was wearing a white turtle-neck sweater, and he towered above the crowd. Reaching for the bullhorn, he began, "Brothers and sisters, we got business to take care of." "Sock soul, brother!" "We got a lot of work to do on this thing, and we gonna march now on over to the church where they're having the rally to help take care of this business." Corky looked stunned. Hosea looked relieved. And the crowd of demonstrators obediently lined up and marched away.

The conflict between the causes of the Mexican-Americans and those of the blacks had come to a head. The relationship had been strained all along, but the S.C.L.C. and Tiejerina had kept it going in the interest of unity and solidarity. Tiejerina's lieutenant, Corky Gonzales, had demanded that Hosea support the demonstration at the Justice Department, and really didn't seem interested in much else. Hosea didn't mind being arrested. In fact, he wanted to be arrested. But this cause—the release in California of a small group of Mexican-Americans charged with conspiracy—just didn't seem broad enough. Corky thought otherwise.

Jackson was not only fresher than Hosea that night—not having been on the demonstration in the hot sun all day—but he was better equipped to deal with Corky, whose orientation was closer to that of the urban hustlers

Jesse Jackson was used to dealing with.

The around-the-clock demonstrations at the Agriculture Department were perhaps the most strenuous ordeals for the demonstrators. More people than usual were asleep during the day at R.C. because they had been up all night sitting on the steps of the Department. And they remained there, regardless of the weather.

One morning, as a weary group stood waiting to be replaced, the sky grew gray and a slight cool wind began to blow. As a heavy downpour of cold rain began, most of the group huddled together under army blankets and started singing.

The last demonstration I attended was on Solidarity Day. In that great mass of 50,000 or more people, I looked for the faces that I had come to know over the last few weeks. I saw only a few, and concluded that the veteran residents of R.C. just happened to be in places that I was not. Later, as the program dragged on and I became weary from the heat, I walked back into the city, expecting to find it empty. Instead I saw the people I had been looking for outside. J.T. and Leon and many others.

Harry Jackson, a cabinet-maker from Baltimore, sat in his usual place—inside the fenced-in compound of the Baltimore delegation. He was keeping watch over the two dormitories—women to the left, men to the right—and a frying pan of baked beans cooking on a small, portable grill. Since he was not out demonstrating, I asked him why he had come to R.C. in the first place. "We came because of the lack of association between the black man and the white man. If the system don't integrate itself, it will segregate itself all over again. Our group was integrated. We had one white fellow from the University of Massachussetts. But he hasn't been back."

This man, I thought, was probably typical of the majority of R.C. residents. They wanted things to get better, and felt that they would if people got together. The system didn't have to come down; it just needed overhauling. Still, the system had created the provincialism and distrust of larger communities that prompted Harry Jackson to remark as I was leaving, "I believe we should keep the people together who came together."

As I walked through Resurrection City, in the distance I could hear the sound of voices coming from the Lincoln Memorial—voices too distant to be understood. After a while, I ran across Leon and J.T. Leon said he was on the way to his A-frame.

"Why aren't you out at the demonstration?" I asked. And barely able to keep his eyes open, he replied weakly, "My demonstration was all night last night. Up at the Agriculture Department. And I'll be there again, all night tonight. That's why I've just got to get some sleep."

A few days later, Jackson and Leon and J.T. and every other resident of Resurrection City were either arrested (for civil disobedience) or tear-gassed (for convenience) by policemen from the District of Columbia. The structures came down in less than half the time it took to put them up. And Resurrection City was dead. Up on the hill, spokesmen for S.C.L.C. said they had achieved some of the goals of the campaign and were making progress toward achieving more. But the people were all—or mostly all—gone.

So, in the end, what did Resurrection City do? It certainly made the poor visible. But did it make them effective? Mr. Abernathy would have them believe that it did. And the people who believed him were, by and large, the ones who had come out of the same area that he had come from. An observer once said that Mr. Abernathy lived for the few hours when he could escape back to his church in Atlanta for Sunday services. This was home. Those who came out of that background were the ones who would have stayed in Washington until their leader said the job was done, working diligently all the while. But they, too, would be glad to get back home.

The confrontations of rural Negroes, not only with officials and the police but with urban blacks as well, may have engendered in them a bit of cynicism—perhaps even a bit of militancy. But one suspects that the talk, for years to come, will be of how they went to Washington and, for all practical purposes, "stood on Eastland's toes."

For the urban-rural types, who were in a transitional position to begin with, the frustrations inherent in the system became only more apparent. Already leaning toward urban-type militancy, their inclinations were reenforced by the treatment that even the nonviolent received when those in control grew weary of them and their cause.

The urban people did not learn anything that they hadn't already known. Except, perhaps, about the differences that exist between them and their Southern brothers. They expected nothing, they gave little, and they got the same in return.

Resurrection City was not really supposed to succeed as a city. It was supposed to succeed in dramatizing the plight of the poor in this country. Instead, its greatest success was in dramatizing what the system has done to the black community in this country. And in doing so, it affirmed the view taken by black militants today—that before black people can make any meaningful progress in the United States of America, they have to, as the militants say, "get themselves together."

October 1968

Rent Strikes:
Poor Man's Weapon

MICHAEL LIPSKY

The poor lack not only money, but power. Low-income political groups may be thought of as politically impoverished. In the bargaining arena of city politics the poor have little to trade.

Protest has come to be an important part of the politics of low-income minorities. By attempting to enlarge the conflict, and bring outside pressures to bear on their concerns, protest has developed as one tactic the poor can use to exert power and gain greater control over their lives. Since the sit-in movement of 1960, Negro civil-rights strategists have used protest to bring about political change, and so have groups associated with the war on poverty. Saul Alinsky's Industrial Areas Foundation continues to receive invitations to help organize low-income communities because it has demonstrated that it can mobilize poor people around the tactics of protest.

The Harlem rent strikes of 1963 and 1964, organized by Jesse Gray, a dynamic black leader who has been agitating about slum housing for more than 15 years, affected some tenants in approximately 150 Harlem tenements. Following the March on Washington in August, 1963, the rent strikes played on the liberal sympathies of New Yorkers who were just beginning to re-examine the conditions of New York City slums. Through a combination of appeal and threat, Jesse Gray mounted a movement that succeeded in changing the orientation of some city services, obtained greater *legal* rights for organized tenants, and resulted in obtaining repairs in a minority of the buildings in which tenants struck. Along with rent strikes conducted by Mobilization for Youth, a pre-war poverty program, the rent strikes managed to project images of thousands of aroused tenants to a concerned public, and to somewhat anxious reform-oriented city officials.

The rent strikes did not succeed in obtaining fundamental goals. Most buildings in which tenants struck remained in disrepair, or deteriorated even further. City housing officials became more responsive to housing problems, but general programs to repair slum housing remained as remote as ever. Perhaps most significant, the rent strike movement, after a hectic initial winter, quickly petered out when cold weather again swept the Harlem streets. Focusing upon the rent strikes may help explain why this protest failed, and why protest in general is not a reliable political weapon.

Protest as a political tactic is limited because protest leaders must appeal to four constituencies at the same time. A protest leader must:

(1) nurture and sustain an organization composed of people who may not always agree with his program or style;

(2) adapt to the mass media—choose strategies and voice goals that will give him as much favorable exposure as possible;

(3) try to develop and sustain the protest's impact on third parties—the general public, sympathetic liberals, or

anyone who can put pressure on those with power; and

(4) try to influence directly the targets of the protest—those who have the power to give him what he wants.

The tensions that result from the leader's need to manipulate four constituencies at once are the basic reason why protest is an unreliable political tactic, unlikely to prove successful in the long run.

Protest activity may be defined as a political activity designed to dramatize an objection to some policies or conditions, using unconventional showmanship or display and aimed at obtaining rewards from the political system while working within that system. The problem of the powerless is that they have little to bargain with, and must acquire resources. Fifteen people sitting in the Mayor's Office cannot, of themselves, hope to move City Hall. But through the publicity they get, or the reaction they evoke, they may politically activate a wider public to which the city administration is sensitive.

The tactic of activating third parties to enter the political process is most important to relatively powerless groups, although it is available to all. Obviously any organization which can call upon a large membership to engage in political activity—a trade union on strike, for example—has some degree of power. But the poor in individual neighborhoods frequently cannot exert such power. Neighborhood political groups may not have mass followings, or may not be able to rely on membership participation in political struggles. In such cases they may be able to activate other political forces in the city to enter the conflict on their behalf. However, the contradictions of the protest process suggest that even this tactic—now widely employed by various low-income groups—cannot be relied upon.

Take, for example, the problem of protest leaders and their constituents. If poor people are to be organized for protest activities, their involvement must be sustained by the symbolic and intangible rewards of participation in protest action, and by the promises of material rewards that protest leaders extend. Yet a leadership style suited to providing protesters with the intangible rewards of participating in rebellious political movements is sometimes incompatible with a style designed to secure tangible benefits for protest group members.

Furthermore, the need of protest leaders to develop a distinctive style in order to overcome the lack of involvement of potential group members diffuses as well as consolidates support. People who want psychological gratification (such as revenge or public notice and acknowledgment), but have little hope of material rewards, will be attracted to a militant leader. They want angry rhetoric and denunciation. On the other hand, those people who depend on the political system for tangible benefits, and therefore believe in it and cooperate with it to some extent, are likely to want moderate leadership. Groups that materially profit from participation in the system will not accept men who question the whole system. Yet the cohesion of relatively powerless groups may be strengthened by militant, ideological leadership that questions the rules of the game, that challenges their morality and legitimacy.

On the other hand, the fact that the sympathies and support of third parties are essential to the success of protesters may make the protesters' fear of retribution, where justified, an asset. For when people put themselves in danger by complaining, they are more likely to gain widespread sympathy. The cattle-prod and police-dog tactics of Alabama police in breaking up demonstrations a few years ago brought immediate response and support from around the country.

In short, the nature of protesters curtails the flexibility of protest leadership. Leaders must limit their public actions to preserve their basis of support. They must also limit protest in line with what they can reasonably expect of their followers. The poor cannot be expected to engage in activities that require much money. The anxieties developed throughout their lives—such as loss of job, fear of police, or danger of eviction—also limit the scope of protest. Negro protest in the South was limited by such retributions or anxieties about facing reprisals.

Jesse Gray was able to gain sympathy for the rent strikers because he was able to project an image of people willing to risk eviction in order to protest against the (rarely identified) slumlords, who exploited them, or the city, whose iceberg pace aided landlords rather than forced them to make repairs. In fact, Gray used an underutilized provision of the law which protected tenants against eviction if they paid their rent to court. It was one of the great strengths of the rent strikes that the image of danger to tenants was projected, while the tenants remained somewhat secure and within the legal process. This fortunate combination is not readily transferable to other cases in which protest activity is contemplated.

Apart from problems relating to manipulation of protest group members, protest leaders must command at least some resources. For instance, skilled professionals must be made available to protest organizations. Lawyers are needed to help protesters use the judicial process, and to handle court cases. The effectiveness of a protest organization may depend upon a combination of an ability to threaten the political system and an ability to exercise legal rights. The organization may either pay lawyers or depend on volunteers. In the case of the rent strikes, dependence on volunteer lawyers was finally abandoned—there were not enough available, and those who were willing could not survive long without payment.

Other professionals may be needed in other protest circumstances. A group trying to protest against an urban-renewal project, for example, will need architects and city planners to present a viable alternative to the city's plan.

Financial resources not only pay lawyers, but allow a minimum program of political activity. In the Harlem rent strikes, dues assessed against the protesters were low and were not collected systematically. Lawyers often complained that tenants were unwilling to pay incidental and minor fees, such as the $2 charge to subpoena departmental records. Obtaining money for mimeo flyers, supplies, rent, telephones, and a small payroll became major problems. The fact that Jesse Gray spent a great deal of time trying to organize new groups, and speaking all over the city, prevented him from paying attention to organizational details. Furthermore, he did not or could not develop assistants who could assume the organizational burden.

Lack of money can sometimes be made up for by passionate support. Lawyers, office help, and block organizers did come forth to work voluntarily for the rent strike. But such help is unreliable and usually transient. When spring came, volunteers vanished rapidly and did not return the following winter. Volunteer assistance usually comes from the more educated and skilled who can get other jobs, at good salaries. The diehards of *ad hoc* political groups are usually those who have no place else to go, nothing else to do.

Lack of money also can be overcome with skilled nonprofessionals; but usually they are scarce. The college students, Negro and white, who staffed the rent-strike offices, handled paper work and press releases, and served as neighborhood organizers, were vital to the strike's success. Not only could they communicate with tenants, but they were relatively sophisticated about the operations of the city government and the communications media. They could help tenants with city agencies, and tell reporters that they wanted to hear. They also maintained contacts with other civil rights and liberal organizations. Other workers might have eventually acquired these skills and contacts, but these student organizers allowed the movement to go into action quickly, on a city-wide scale, and with a large volume of cases. One of the casualties of "black power" has been the exclusion of skilled white college students from potentially useful roles of this kind.

Like the proverbial tree that falls unheard in the forest,

protest, politically speaking, does not exist unless it is projected and perceived. To the extent that a successful protest depends on appealing to, or perhaps also threatening, other groups in the community, publicity through the public media will set the limits of how far that protest activity will go toward success. (A number of writers, in fact, have noticed that the success of a protest seems directly related to publicity outside the immediate protest area.) If the communications media either ignore the protest or play it down, it will not succeed.

When the protest *is* covered, the way it is given publicity will influence all participants including the protesters themselves. Therefore, it is vital that a leader know what the media consider newsworthy, and be familiar with the prejudices and desires of those who determine what is to be covered and how much.

But media requirements are often contradictory and hard to meet. TV wants spot news, perhaps 30 seconds' worth; newspapers want somewhat more than that, and long stories may appear only in weekly neighborhood or ethnic papers. Reporters want topical newsworthiness in the short run—the more exciting the better. They will even stretch to get it. But after that they want evidence, accuracy, and reliability. The leader who was too accommodating in the beginning may come to be portrayed as an irresponsible liar.

This conflict was well illustrated in the rent strike. Jesse Gray and the reporters developed an almost symbiotic relationship. They wanted fresh, dramatic news on the growth of the strike—and Gray was happy to give them progress reports he did not, and could not, substantiate.

Actually, just keeping the strikes going in a limited number of buildings would have been a considerable feat. Yet reporters wanted more than that—they wanted growth. Gray, of course, had other reasons for reporting that the strike was spreading—he knew that such reports, if believed, would help pressure city officials. In misrepresenting the facts, Gray was encouraged by sympathetic reporters—in the long run actually undermining his case. As a *New York Times* reporter explained, "We had an interest in keeping it going."

Having encouraged Gray to go out on a limb and overstate the support he had, the reporters later were just as eager for documentation. It was not forthcoming. Gray consistently failed to produce a reliable list of rent-strike buildings that could withstand independent verification. He took the reporters only to those buildings he considered "safe." And the newspapers that had themselves strongly contributed to the inflation of Gray's claims then helped deflate them and denied him press coverage.

The clash between the needs of these two constituencies —the media and the protesters—often puts great strain on leaders. The old-line leader who appeals to his followers because of his apparent responsibility, integrity, and restraint will not capture the necessary headlines. On the other hand, the leader who finds militant rhetoric a useful weapon for organizing some people will find the media only too eager to carry his more inflammatory statements. But this portrayal of him as an uncompromising firebrand (often meant for a limited audience and as a limited tactic) will alienate him from people he may need for broad support, and may work toward excluding him from bargaining with city officials.

If a leader takes strong or extreme positions, he may win followers and newspaper space, but alienate the protest's target. Exclusion from the councils of bargaining or decision-making can have serious consequences for protest leaders, since the targets can then concentrate on satisfying the aroused public and civic groups, while ignoring the demands of the protesters.

What a protest leader must do to get support from third parties will also often conflict with what he must do to retain the interest and support of his followers. For instance, when Negro leaders actually engage in direct bargaining with politicians, they may find their supporters outraged or discouraged, and slipping away. They need militancy to arouse support; they need support to bargain; but if they bargain, they may seem to betray that militancy, and lose support. Yet bargaining at some point may be necessary to obtain objectives from city politicians. These tensions can be minimized to some extent by a protest organization's having divided leadership. One leader may bargain with city officials, while another continues rhetorical guerilla warfare.

Divided leadership may also prove useful in solving the problem that James Q. Wilson has noted: "The militant displays an unwillingness to perform those administrative tasks which are necessary to operate an organization." The nuts and bolts of administrative detail are vital. If protest depends primarily on a leader's charisma, as the rent strikes did to some extent, allocating responsibility (already difficult because of lack of skilled personnel) can become a major problem. In the rent strike, somebody had to coordinate court appearances for tenants and lawyers; somebody had to subpoena Building and Health Department records and collect money to pay for them; and somebody had to be alert to the fact that, through landlord duplicity or tenant neglect, tenants might face immediate eviction and require emergency legal assistance. Jesse Gray was often unable, or unwilling, to concentrate of these details. In part failures of these kinds are forced on the protest leader, who must give higher priority to publicity and arousing support than to administrative detail. However, divided leadership can help separate responsibility for administration from responsibility for mobilization.

Strain between militancy to gain and maintain support and reasonableness to obtain concessions can also be diminished by successful "public relations." Protest groups may understand the same words differently than city officials. Imperatives to march or burn are usually not the commands frightened whites sometimes think they are.

Protest success depends partly upon enlarging the number of groups and individuals who are concerned about the issues. It also depends upon ability to influence the shape of the decision, not merely whether or not there will be a decision. This is one reason why protest is more likely to succeed when groups are trying to veto a decision (say, to stop construction of an expressway), than when they try to initiate projects (say, to establish low-cost transportation systems for a neighborhood).

Protest groups are often excluded from the bargaining arena because the civic groups and city officials who make decisions in various policy areas have developed relationships over long periods of time, for mutual benefit. Interlopers are not admitted to these councils easily. Men in power do not like to sit down with people they consider rogues. They do not seek the dubious pleasure of being denounced, and are uneasy in the presence of people whose class, race, or manners are unfamiliar. They may make opportunities available for "consultation," or even "confrontation," but decisions will be made behind closed doors where the nature of the decision is not open to discussion by "outsiders."

As noted before, relatively powerless protest groups seldom have enough people of high status to work for their proposals. Good causes sometimes attract such people, but seldom for long. Therefore protest groups hardly ever have the expertise and experience they need, including professionals in such fields as law, architecture, accounting, education, and how to get government money. This is one area in which the "political impoverishment" of low-income groups is most clearly observed. Protest groups may learn how to dramatize issues, but they cannot present data or proposals that public officials consider "objective" or "reasonable." Few men can be both passionate advocate and persuasive arbiter at the same time.

Ultimately the success of a protest depends on the targets.

Many of the forces that inhibit protest leaders from influencing target groups have already been mentioned: the protesters' lack of status, experience, and resources in bargaining; the conflict between the rhetoric that will inspire and hold supporters, and what will open the door to meaningful bargaining; conflicting press demands, and so on.

But there is an additional factor that constrains protest organizations that deal with public agencies. As many students of organizations have pointed out, public agencies and the men who run them are concerned with maintaining and enhancing the agency's position. This means protecting the agency from criticism and budget cuts, and attempting to increase the agency's status and scope. This piece of conventional wisdom has great importance for a protest group which can only succeed by getting others to apply pressure on public policy. Public agencies are most responsive to their regular critics and immediate organizational allies. Thus if they can deflect pressure from these, their reference groups, they can ease the pressure brought by protest *without meeting any of the protest demands.*

At least six tactics are available to targets that are inclined to respond in some way to protests. They may respond with symbolic satisfactions. Typical, in city politics, is the ribbon-cutting, street-corner ceremony, or the Mayor's walking press conference. When tension builds up in Harlem, Mayor Lindsay walks the streets and talks to the people. Such occasions are not only used to build support, but to persuade the residents that attention is being directed to their problems.

City agencies establish special machinery and procedures to prepare symbolic means for handling protest crises. For instance, in those New York departments having to do with housing, top officials, a press secretary, and one or two others will devote whatever time is necessary to collecting information and responding quickly to reporters' inquiries about a developing crisis. This is useful for tenants: It means that if they can create enough concern, they can cut through red tape. It is also useful for officials who want to appear ready to take action.

During the New York rent strikes, city officials responded by: initiating an anti-rat campaign; proposing ways to "legalize" rent strikes (already legal under certain conditions) ; starting a program to permit the city to make repairs; and contracting for a costly university study to review housing code enforcement procedures. Some of these steps were of distinct advantage to tenants, although none was directed at the overall slum problem. It is important to note, however, that the announcement of these programs served to deflect pressure by reassuring civic groups and a liberal public that something was being done. Regardless of how well-meaning public officials are, real changes in conditions are secondary to the general agency need to develop a response to protest that will "take the heat off."

■ Another tactic available to public officials is to give token satisfactions. When city officials respond, with much publicity, to a few cases brought to them, they can appear to be meeting protest demands, while actually meeting only those few cases. If a child is bitten by a rat, and enough hue and cry is raised, the rats in that apartment or building may be exterminated, with much fanfare. The building next door remains infested.

Such tokenism may give the appearance of great improvement, while actually impeding real overall progress by alleviating public concern. Tokenism is particularly attractive to reporters and television news directors, who are able to dramatize individual cases convincingly. General situations are notoriously hard to dramatize.

■ To blunt protest drives, protest targets may also work to change their internal procedures and organization. This tactic is similar to the preceding one. By developing means to concentrate on those cases that are most dramatic, or seem to pose the greatest threats, city officials can effectively wear down the cutting-edges of protest.

As noted, all New York City agencies have informal arrangements to deal with such crisis cases. During the rent strikes two new programs were developed by the city whereby officials could enter buildings to make repairs and exterminate rats on an emergency basis. Previously, officials had been confined to trying to find the landlords and to taking them to court (a time-consuming, ineffective process that has been almost universally criticized by knowledgeable observers). These new programs were highly significant developments because they expanded the scope of governmental responsibility. They acknowledged, in a sense, that slum conditions are a social disease requiring public intervention.

At the same time, these innovations served the purposes of administrators who needed the power to make repairs in the worst housing cases. If public officials can act quickly in the most desperate situations that come to their attention, pressure for more general attacks on housing problems can be deflected.

The new programs could never significantly affect the 800,000 deteriorating apartments in New York City. The new programs can operate only so long as the number of crises are relatively limited. Crisis treatment for everyone would mean shifting resources from routine services. If all cases receive priority, then none can.

The new programs, however welcomed by some individual tenants, help agencies to "cool off" crises quicker. This also may be the function of police review boards and internal complaint bureaus. Problems can be handled more expeditiously with such mechanisms while agency personnel behavior remains unaffected.

■ Target groups may plead that their hands are tied—because of laws or stubborn superiors, or lack of resources or authority. They may be sympathetic, but what can they do? Besides, "If-I-give-it-to-you-I-have-to-give-it-to-everyone."

Illustratively, at various times during the rent strike, city officials claimed they did not have funds for emergency repairs (although they found funds later), and lacked authority to enter buildings to make emergency repairs (although the city later acted to make emergency repairs under provisions of a law available for over 60 years). This tactic is persuasive; everyone knows that cities are broke, and limited by state law. But if pressure rises, funds for specific, relatively inexpensive programs, or expansion of existing programs, can often be found.

■ Targets may use their extensive resources and contacts to discredit protest leaders and organizations: "They don't really have the people behind them"; they are acting "criminally"; they are "left-wing." These allegations can cool the sympathies of the vital third parties, whether or not there is any truth behind them. City officials, especially, can use this device in their contacts with civic groups and communication media, with which they are mutually dependent for support and assistance. Some city officials can downgrade protesters while others appear sympathetic to the protesters' demands.

■ Finally, target groups may postpone action—time is on their side. Public sympathy cools quickly, and issues are soon forgotten. Moreover, because low-income protest groups have difficulty sustaining organization (for reasons suggested above), they are particularly affected by delays. The threat represented by protest dissipates with time, the difficulty of managing for constituencies increases as more and more information circulates, and the inherent instability of protest groups makes it unlikely that they will be able to take effective action when decisions are finally announced.

The best way to procrastinate is to commit the subject to "study." By the time the study is ready, if ever, the protest group will probably not be around to criticize or press for implementation of proposals. The higher the status of the study group, the less capable low-status protest groups will be able to effectively challenge the final product. Furthermore, officials retain the option of rejecting or failing to accept the reports of study groups, a practice developed to an art by the Johnson administration.

This is not to say that surveys, research and study groups are to be identified solely as delaying tactics. They are often desirable, even necessary, to document need and mobilize public and pressure group support. But postponement, for whatever reason, will always change the pressures on policy-makers, usually in directions unfavorable to protest results.

Groups without power can attempt to gain influence through protest. I have argued that protest will be successful to the extent that the protesters can get third parties to put pressure on the targets. But protest leaders have severe problems in trying to meet the needs and desires of four separate and often conflicting constituencies—their supporters, the mass media, the interested and vital third parties, and the targets of the protest.

By definition, relatively powerless groups have few resources, and therefore little probability of success. But to survive at all and to arouse the third parties, they need at least some resources. Even to get these minimal resources, conflicting demands limit the leader's effectiveness. And when, finally, public officials are forced to recognize protest activity, it is not to meet the demands, but to satisfy other groups that have influence.

Edelman has written that, in practice, regulatory policy consists of reassuring mass publics symbolically while at the same time dispensing tangible concessions only to narrow interest groups. Complementing Edelman, I have suggested that public officials give symbolic reassurances to protest groups, rather than real concessions, because those on whom they most depend will be satisfied with appearances of action. Rent strikers wanted to see repairs in their apartments and dramatic improvements in slum housing; but the wider publics that most influence city officials could be satisfied simply by the appearance of reform. And when city officials had satisfied the publics this way, they could then resist or ignore the protesters' demands for other or more profound changes.

Kenneth Clark, in *Dark Ghetto,* has observed that the illusion of having power, when unaccompanied by material rewards, leads to feelings of helplessness and reinforces political apathy in the ghetto. If the poor and politically weak protest to acquire influence that will help change their lives and conditions, only to find that little comes from all that risk and trouble, then apathy or hostility toward conventional political methods may result.

If the arguments presented in this article are convincing, then those militant civil-rights leaders who insist that protest is a shallow foundation on which to build longterm, concrete gains are essentially correct. But their accompanying arguments—the fickleness of the white liberal, the difficulty of changing discriminatory institutions as opposed to discriminatory laws—are only part of the explanation for the essential failure of protest. An analysis of the politics involved strongly suggests that protest is best understood by concentrating on problems of managing diverse protest constituencies.

It may be, therefore, that Saul Alinsky is on soundest ground when he recommends protest as a tactic to build an organization, which can then command its own power. Protest also may be recommended to increase or change the political consciousness of people, or to gain short run goals in a potentially sympathetic political environment. This may be the most significant contribution of the black power movement—the development of group consciousness which provides a more cohesive political base. But ultimately relatively powerless groups cannot rely on the protest process alone to help them obtain long-run goals, or general improvements in conditions. What they need for long-run success are stable political resources—in a word, power. The American political system is theoretically open; but it is closed, for many reasons suggested here, to politically impoverished groups. While politicians continue to affirm the right to dissent or protest within reason, the political process in which protest takes place remains highly restricted.

February 1969

FURTHER READING SUGGESTED BY THE AUTHOR:

Dark Ghetto: Dilemmas of Social Power by Kenneth B. Clark (New York: Harper and Row, 1965), explores the implications of powerlessness in the ghetto on the psychology of individuals and on the viability of political movements.

Neighborhood Groups and Urban Renewal by J. Clarence Davies, III (New York: Columbia University Press, 1966). One of the few systematic studies of the interaction of political organizations and city agencies at the neighborhood level.

The Symbolic Uses of Politics, by Murray Edelman (Urbana, Illinois: University of Illinois Press, 1964) is a highly suggestive study of the symbolic meaning of government activity and the ways such activity affects political consciousness and activism.

Sniping -
New Pattern of Violence?

TERRY ANN KNOPF

On July 23, 1968, at 2:15 P.M., Cleveland's Mayor, Carl
B. Stokes, who was in Washington, D.C., that day, made
what he expected to be a routine telephone call to his office back home. He was told of information from military,
F.B.I., and local police intelligence sources indicating that
an armed uprising by black militants was scheduled to take
place at 8 A.M. the next day. According to the reports,
Ahmed Evans, a militant leader who headed a group
called the Black Nationalists of New Libya, planned to
drive to Detroit that night to secure automatic weapons.
There were further reports that Evans' followers had already purchased bandoliers, ammunition pouches, and first-
aid kits that same day. Simultaneous uprisings were reportedly being planned for Detroit, Pittsburgh, and Chicago.

At 6 P.M., in response to these reports, several un-
marked police cars were assigned to the area of Evans'

47

house. At about 8:20 P.M. a group of armed men, some of whom were wearing bandoliers of ammunition, emerged from the house. Almost at once, an intense gun battle broke out between the police and the armed men, lasting for roughly an hour. A second gun battle between the police and snipers broke out shortly after midnight about 40 blocks away. In the wake of these shoot-outs, sporadic looting and firebombing erupted and continued for several days. By the time the disorder was over, 16,400 National Guardsmen had been mobilized, at least nine persons had been killed (including three policemen), while the property damage was estimated at $1.5 million. Police listed most of their casualties as "shot by sniper."

Immediately, the Cleveland tragedy was described as a deliberate plot against the police and said to signal a new phase in the current course of racial conflict. *The Cleveland Press* (July 24, 1968) compared the violence in Cleveland to guerrilla activity in Saigon and noted: ". . . It didn't seem to be a Watts, or a Detroit, or a Newark. Or even a Hough of two years ago. No, this tragic night seemed to be part of a plan." Thomas A. Johnson writing in *The New York Times* (July 28, 1968) stated: ". . . It marks perhaps the first documented case in recent history of black, armed, and organized violence against the police."

As the notion that police were being "ambushed" took hold in the public's mind, many observers reporting on the events in Cleveland and similar confrontations in other cities, such as Gary, Peoria, Seattle, and York, Pennsylvania, emphasized that the outbreaks had several prominent features in common.

The first was the element of planning. Racial outbursts have traditionally been spontaneous affairs, without organization and without leadership. While no two disorders are similar in every respect, studies conducted in the past have indicated that a riot is a dynamic process that goes through stages of development. John P. Spiegel of Brandeis' Lemberg Center for the Study of Violence, has discerned four stages in the usual sort of rioting: the precipitating event, street confrontation, "Roman holiday," and seige. A sequence of stages is outlined in somewhat similar terms in the section of the Kerner Report on "the riot process." It is significant, however, that neither the Lemberg Center nor the Kerner Commission found any evidence of an organized plan or "conspiracy" in civil disorders prior to 1968. According to the Kerner Report: ". . . The Commission has found no evidence that all or any of the disorders or the incidents that led to them were planned or directed by any organization or group—international, national, or local."

Since the Cleveland shoot-out, however, many observers have suggested that civil disorders are beginning to take a new form, characterized by some degree of planning, organization, and leadership.

The second new feature discerned in many of 1968's summer outbreaks was the attacks on the police. In the past, much of the racial violence that occurred was directed at property rather than persons. Cars were stoned, stores were looted, business establishments were firebombed, and residences, in some instances, were damaged or destroyed. However, since the Cleveland gun battle, there have been suggestions that policemen have become the primary targets of violence. A rising curve of ambushes of the police was noted in the October 7, 1968 issue of the *U.S. News & World Report* which maintained that at least 8 policemen were killed and 47 wounded in such attacks last summer.

Finally, attacks on the police are now said to be *regularly* characterized by hit-and-run sniping. Using either home-made weapons or commercial and military weapons, such as automatics, bands of snipers are pictured initiating guerrilla warfare in our cities.

This view of the changing nature of racial violence can be found across a broad spectrum of the press, ranging from the moderately liberal *New York Times* to the miltantly rightist *American Opinion.* On August 3, 1968, *The New York Times* suggested in an editorial:

> . . . The pattern in 1967 has not proved to be the pattern of 1968. Instead of violence almost haphazardly exploding, it has sometimes been deliberately planned. And while the 1967 disorders served to rip away false facades of racial progress and expose rusting junkyards of broken promises, the 1968 disorders also reveal a festering militancy that prompts some to resort to open warfare.

Shortly afterward (August 14, 1968), *Crime Control Digest,* a biweekly periodical read by many law-enforcement officials across the country, declared:

> The pattern of civil disorders in 1968 has changed from the pattern that prevailed in 1967, and the elaborate U.S. Army, National Guard and police riot control program prepared to meet this year's "long hot summer" will have to be changed if this year's type of civil disturbance is to be prevented or controlled.
>
> This year's riot tactics have featured sniping and hit-and-run attacks on the police, principally by Black Power extremists, but by teen-agers in an increasing number of instances. The type of crimes being committed by the teen-agers and the vast increase in their participation has already brought demands that they be tried and punished as adults.

On September 13, 1968, *Time* took note of an "ominous trend" in the country:

Violence as a form of Negro protest appears to be changing from the spontaneous combustion of a mob to the premeditated shoot-outs of a far-out few. Many battles have started with well-planned sniping at police. Predictably, the November 1968 issue of *American Opinion* went beyond the other accounts by linking reported attacks on the police to a Communist plot:

The opening shots of the Communists' long-planned terror offensive against our local police were fired in Cleveland on the night of July 23, 1968, when the city's Glenville area rattled with the scream of automatic weapons. . . . What happened in Cleveland, alas, was only a beginning.

To further emphasize the point, a large headline crying "terrorism" was included on the cover of the November issue.

Despite its relative lack of objectivity, *American Opinion* is the only publication that has attempted to list sniping incidents. Twenty-five specific instances of attacks on police were cited in the November issue. Virtually every other publication claiming a change in the nature of racial violence pointing to the "scores of American cities" affected and the "many battles" between blacks and the police has confined itself to a few perfunctory examples as evidence. Even when a few examples have been offered, the reporters usually have not attempted to investigate and confirm them.

Without attempting an exhaustive survey, we at the Lemberg Center were able to collect local and national press clippings, as well as wire-service stories, that described 25 separate incidents of racial violence in July and August of last summer. In all these stories, sniping was alleged to have taken place at some point or other in the fracas, and in most of them, the police were alleged to have been the primary targets of the sharpshooters. Often, too, the reports held that evidence had been found of planning on the part of "urban guerrillas," and at times it was claimed that the police had been deliberately ambushed. Needless to say, the specter of the Black Panthers haunts a number of the accounts. Throughout, one finds such phrases as these: "snipers hidden behind bushes . . . ," "isolated sniper fire . . . ," "scattered sniping directed at the police . . . ," "exchange of gunfire between snipers and police . . . ," "snipers atop buildings in the area. . . ." It is small wonder that the rewrite men at *Time* and other national magazines discerned a new and sinister pattern in the events of that summer. Small wonder that many concerned observers are convinced that the country's racial agony has entered a new phase of deliberate covert violence.

But how valid is this sometimes conspiratorial, sometimes apocalyptic view? What is the evidence for it, apart from these newspaper accounts?

Our assessment is based on an analysis of newspaper clippings, including a comparison of initial and subsequent reports, local and national press coverage, and on telephone interviews with high-ranking police officials. The selection of police officials was deliberate on our part. In the absence of city or state investigations of most of the incidents, police departments were found to be the best (and in many cases the only) source of information. Moreover, as the reported targets of sniping, police officials understandably had a direct interest in the subject.

Of course, the selection of this group did involve an element of risk. A tendency of some police officials to exaggerate and inflate sniping reports was thought to be unavoidable. We felt, though, that every group involved would have a certain bias and that in the absence of interviewing every important group in the cities, the views of police officials were potentially the most illuminating and therefore the most useful. Our interviews with them aimed at the following points: 1) evidence of planning; 2) the number of snipers; 3) the number of shots fired; 4) affiliation of the sniper or snipers with an organization; 5) statistical breakdowns of police and civilian casualties by sniping; and 6) press coverage of the incident.

As the press reports showed, a central feature in the scheme of those alleging a new pattern involves the notion of planning. Hypothesizing a local (if not national) conspiracy, observers have pictured black militants luring the police to predetermined spots where the policemen become the defenseless victims of an armed attack. No precipitating incident is involved in these cases except perhaps for a false citizen's call.

Despite this view, the information we gathered indicates that at least 17 out of the 25 disorders surveyed (about 70 percent) *did* begin with an identifiable precipitating event (such as an arrest seen by the black community as insulting or unjust) similar to those uncovered for "traditional" disorders. The figure of 70 percent is entirely consistent with the percentage of known precipitating incidents isolated by researchers at the Lemberg Center for past disorders (also about 70 percent).

In Gary, Indiana, the alleged sniping began shortly after two young members of a gang were arrested on charges of rape. In York, Pennsylvania, the violence began after a white man fired a shotgun from his apartment at some blacks on the street. Blacks were reportedly angered upon learning that the police had failed to arrest the gunman. In Peoria, Illinois, police arrested a couple for creating a disturbance in a predominantly black housing-project area. A group of young people then appeared on the scene and began throwing missiles at the police. In Seattle, Washington, a disturbance erupted shortly after a rally was held to protest the arrest of two men at the local Black Panther headquarters. Yet the disorders that followed these incidents are among the most prominently mentioned as examples of planned violence.

Many of the precipitating events were tied to the actions of the police and in some instances they were what the Kerner Commission has referred to as "tension-heightening incidents," meaning that the incident (or the disorder itself) merely crystallized tensions already existing in the community. Shortly before an outbreak in Harvey-Dixmoor, Illinois, on August 6–7, for example, a coroner's jury had ruled that the fatal shooting by police of a young, suspected car thief one month earlier was justifiable homicide. It was the second time in four months that a local policeman had shot a black youth. In Miami, the rally held by blacks shortly before the violence erupted coincided with the Republican National Convention being held about 10 miles away. The crowd was reportedly disappointed when the Reverend Ralph Abernathy and basketball star Wilt Chamberlain failed to appear as announced. In addition, tensions had risen in recent months following increased police canine patrols in the area. Although no immediate precipitating incident was uncovered for the outbreak at Jackson, Michigan on August 5, it is noteworthy that the disorder occurred in front of a Catholic-sponsored center aimed at promoting better race relations, and several weeks earlier, some 30 blacks had attempted to take over the center in the name of "a black group run by black people."

Let us turn briefly to the eight disorders in which triggering events do not appear to have occurred. Despite the absence of such an incident in the Chicago Heights-

East Chicago Heights disorder, Chief of Police Robert A. Stone (East Chicago Heights) and Captain Jack Ziegler (Chicago Heights) indicated that they had no evidence of planning and that the disorder was in all probability spontaneous. In particular, Chief Stone indicated that the participants were individuals rather than members of an organization. The same holds true for the "ambuscade" in Brooklyn, New York, which the district attorney said at the time was the work of the Black Panthers. Although no precipitating event was uncovered, R. Harcourt Dodds, Deputy Commissioner for Legal Matters in the New York City Police Department, indicated there was no evidence of planning by anyone or any group. In Jackson, Michigan, as previously noted, tensions in the community had increased in recent weeks prior to the August disorder over a controversial center which some members of the community thought they should control. Thus the absence of precipitating events in at least three cases does not appear to be significant, least of all as evidence of a deliberate conspiracy to kill.

An assessment of the other five cases is considerably more difficult. In Inkster, Michigan, where four nights of isolated sniper fire were reported in August, Chief of Police James L. Fyke did not identify any precipitating event with the disorder and indicated that the state planned to make a case for conspiracy at a forthcoming trial. On the grounds that the two disorders in his city were under police investigation, Lieutenant Norman H. Judd of the Los Angeles Police Department declined comment on possible triggering events. In San Francisco, Chief of Police Thomas J. Cahill said there was evidence of planning. He said that "a firebomb was ignited and the shots were fired as the police vehicle arrived at the scene."

This brings us to Cleveland and Ahmed Evans, the

fifth case in this instance. Because of the dramatic nature of the events and the tremendous amount of attention they received in the national press, any findings concerning Cleveland are of utmost importance. It is significant, therefore, that more recent reports have revealed that the July bloodletting was something less than a planned uprising and that the situation at the time was considerably more complicated than indicated initially.

A series of articles appearing in *The New York Times* is instructive. At the time of the disorder, in an account by Thomas A. Johnson, entitled "This Was Real Revolution," *The New York Times* gave strong hints of a plot against the police: "Early indications here were that a small, angry band of Negro men decided to shoot it out with the police. . . ." The article dwelt upon past statements of Ahmed Evans predicting armed uprisings across the nation on May 9, 1967 (they never materialized), rumors of arms caches across the country, and the revolutionary talk of black militants. No mention was made of any precipitating event, nor was there any reference to "tension-heightening incidents" in the community at the time.

One month later, in early September, *The New York Times* published the results of its investigation of the disorder. The report was prepared by three newsmen, all of whom had covered the disorder earlier. Their findings shed new light on the case by suggesting that a series of tension-heightening factors were indeed present in the community at the time of the disorder. For one thing, Mayor Stokes attended a meeting with police officials several hours before the first outbreak and felt that the information about a planned uprising was "probably not correct." Ahmed Evans himself was seen, retrospectively, less as the mastermind of a plot than as just another militant. Anthony

Ripley of *The New York Times* wrote of him: "Evans, a tall, former Army Ranger who had been dishonorably discharged after striking an officer, was not regarded as a leading black nationalist. He was an amateur astrologer, 40 years old, given more to angry speeches than to action." Numerous grievances in the community—particularly against the police—which had been overlooked at the time of the disorder, were cited later. For example, it was noted that there were only 165 blacks on a police force of more than 2,000 officers, and there was a deep resentment felt by blacks toward their treatment by the police. The reporters also turned up the fact that in 1966 an investigation committee had given a low professional rating to the police department.

Ahmed Evans himself had some more specific grievances, according to Thomas A. Johnson's follow-up article. He noted that Evans had arranged to rent a vacant tavern for the purpose of teaching the manufacture of African-style clothes and carvings to black youths but that the white landlady had changed her mind. He said that Evans had been further angered upon receiving an eviction order from his home. The Ripley article noted that, two hours before the shooting began, Evans said he had been asleep until his associates informed him that police surveillance cars had been stationed in the area. (Evans was accustomed to posting lookouts on top of buildings.) According to Evans, it was then that the group made the decision to arm.

Did the presence of the police in the area serve to trigger the gun battle that followed? What was the role of the civilian tow-truck driver wearing a police-like uniform? Did his hitching up an old pink Cadillac heighten tensions to the breaking point? Were intelligence reports of a plot in error? Why were arms so readily available to the group? What was the group's intention upon emerging from the house? These questions cannot be answered with any degree of absolute certainty. Nevertheless, it is significant that the earliest interpretations appearing in *The New York Times* were greatly modified by the subsequent articles revealing the complexities of the disorder and suggesting it may have been more spontaneous than planned. As Ripley wrote in his September 2 article:

> The Cleveland explosion has been called both an ambush of police and an armed uprising by Negroes. However, the weight of evidence indicates that it was closer to spontaneous combustion.

More recent developments on the controversial Cleveland case deserve mention also. On May 12, 1969, an all-white jury found Ahmed Evans guilty of seven counts of first-degree murder arising out of four slayings during the disorder last July. Evans was sentenced to die in the electric chair on September 22, 1969.

Then, on May 29, 1969, the National Commission on the Causes and Prevention of Violence authorized the release of a report entitled *Shoot-Out in Cleveland; Black Militants and the Police: July 23, 1968* by Louis H. Masotti and Jerome R. Corsi. The report was partially underwritten by the Lemberg Center. Its findings confirmed many of the results of *The Times* investigation and provided additional insights into the case.

Doubt was cast on prior intelligence reports that the Evans group had been assembling an arsenal of handguns and carbines, that Evans planned a trip to Detroit to secure weapons, and that simultaneous outbreaks in other northern cities were planned. ("The truth of these reports was questionable.") Further, it was revealed that these reports came from a single individual and that "other intelligence sources did not corroborate his story." In addition, the Commission report underscored certain provocative actions by the police:

It was glaringly evident that the police had established a stationary surveillance rather than a moving one. In fact, another surveillance car was facing Ahmed's apartment building from the opposite direction. . . . Both cars contained only white officers; both were in plain view of Ahmed's home. . . . Rightly or wrongly, Ahmed regarded the obvious presence of the surveillance cars over several hours' time as threatening.

The report stressed that "against theories of an ambush or well-planned conspiracy stands the evidence that on Tuesday evening [July 23, 1968] Ahmed was annoyed and apprehensive about the police surveillance."

The Times experience, together with the report of the National Commission on the Causes and Prevention of Violence, strongly suggest that the assumption that the Cleveland disorder was planned is as yet unproved.

It may be significant that 14 out of the 19 police officials who expressed a view on the matter could find no evidence of planning in the disorders in their respective cities. In another instance, the police official said the disorder was planned, but he could offer no evidence in support of his statement. If this and the Cleveland case are been planned comes to at least 16 out of 19.

In their assertions that police are now the principal targets of snipers, some observers give the impression that there have been large numbers of police casualties. In most cases, the reports have not been explicit in stating figures. However, as mentioned earlier, *U.S. News & World Report* cited 8 police deaths and 47 police woundings this past summer. In order to assess these reports, we obtained from police officials a breakdown of police casualties as a result of gunfire.

What we learned was that a total of four policemen were killed and that each death was by gunfire. But three of these occurred in one city, Cleveland; the other was in Inkster, Michigan. In other words, in 23 out of 25 cases where sniping was originally reported, no policemen were killed.

Police Casualties

Our total agreed with figures initially taken from local press reports. However, our count of four dead was only half the figure reported in *U.S. News & World Report.* We learned why when we found that the story appearing in that magazine originally came from an Associated Press "roundup," which said that eight policemen had been killed by gunfire since July 1, 1968. But four of these eight cases were in the nature of individual acts of purely criminal—and not racial—violence. On July 2, a Washington, D.C., policeman was killed when he tried to arrest a man on a robbery complaint. A Philadelphia policeman was killed July 15 while investigating a $59 streetcar robbery. On August 5, in San Antonio, a policeman was killed by a 14-year-old boy he had arrested. The youth was a Mexican-American who had been arrested on a drinking charge. And, in Detroit, a policeman was shot to death on August 5 following a domestic quarrel. The circumstances concerning these four cases in no way display the features of a "new pattern" of violence.

The question of how many police *injuries* came from sniper fire is more complicated. A total of 92 policemen were injured, accounting for 14 out of 25 cases. Almost half the injuries—44—came from gunfire. In some instances, our findings showed a downward revision of our earlier information. In Gary, for example, somebody reportedly took a shot at Police Chief James F. Hilton as he cruised the troubled area shortly after the disturbance began. However, when interviewed, Chief Hilton vigorously denied the earlier report. In Peoria, 11 police officers were reportedly injured by shotgun blasts. However, Bernard J. Kennedy, Director of Public Safety, indicated that initial reports "were highly exaggerated" and that only seven officers were actually wounded. In East Point, Georgia, a white policeman had reportedly been injured during the disorder. Yet Acting Police Chief Hugh D. Brown indicated that there were no injuries to the police. In Little Rock, a policeman swore that he had been shot by a sniper. However, Chief of Police R. E. Brians told us that there was no injury and no broken skin. The Chief added that the policeman had been new and was not of the highest caliber. In fact, he is no longer with the department.

In addition, a closer look at the data reveals that the highest figures for numbers of policemen wounded by gunfire are misleading and need to be placed in perspective. Let us examine the three cases with the highest number of injuries: Cleveland with 10 policemen wounded by gunfire; Peoria, with seven; and Harvey-Dixmoor, Illinois, also with seven.

In Peoria, all seven policemen were wounded by the pellets from *a single shotgun blast.* In an interview, Safety Director Kennedy stressed that "none of the injuries incurred were serious." The Harvey-Dixmoor incident was similar. There, five out of the seven injured were also hit by a single shotgun blast. Chief of Police Leroy H. Knapp Jr. informed us that only two or three shots were fired during the entire disorder. (A similar scattering of pellets occurred in St. Paul, where three out of four policemen hit by gunfire received their injuries from one shotgun blast.)

In Cleveland, almost every injury to a policeman came as a result of gunfire. However, it is not at all clear whether snipers inflicted the damage. In the chaos that accompanies many disorders, shots have sometimes been fired accidentally—by both rioters and policemen. Ripley's September 2 article in *The New York Times* stated the problem very well: "Only by setting the exact position of each man when he was shot, tracing the bullet paths, and locating all other policemen at the scene can a reasonable answer be found." Thus far, no information concerning the circumstances of each casualty in the Cleveland disorder has been disclosed, and this goes for deaths as well as injuries.

Moreover, what applies to Cleveland applies to the other disorders as well. The Little Rock case illustrates the point. Chief of Police Brians verified the shooting of a National Guardsman. However, he also clarified the circumstances of the shooting. He said that during the disorder a group of people gathered on a patio above a courtyard near the area where the National Guard was stationed. One individual, under the influence of alcohol, fired indiscriminantly into the crowd, hitting a guardsman in the foot. Chief Brians added: "He might just as easily have hit a [civil-rights] protestor as a guardsman." What is clear is that the circumstances concerning all casualties need to be clarified so as to avoid faulty inferences and incorrect judgments as much as possible.

Concerning the amount of sniping, there were numerous discrepancies between early and later reports, suggesting that many initial reports were exaggerated.

According to the police officials themselves, other than in the case of Cleveland where 25 to 30 snipers were allegedly involved, there were relatively few snipers. In 15 out of 17 cases where such information was available, police officials said there were three snipers or less. And in 7 out of 17 cases, the officials directly contradicted press reports at the time and said that no snipers were involved!

As for the number of gunshots fired by snipers, the reality, as reported by police, was again a lot less exciting than the newspapers indicated. In 15 out of 18 cases where information was available, "snipers" fired fewer than 10 shots. In 12 out of 18 cases, snipers fired fewer than five. Generally, then, in more than one-quarter of the cases in which sniping was originally reported, later indications were that no sniping had actually occurred.

In Evansville, initial reports indicated that a minimum of eight shots were fired. Yet Assistant Chief of Police Charles M. Gash told us that only one shot was fired.

A more dramatic illustration is found in the case of East Point, Georgia. Although 50 shots were reportedly fired at the time, Acting Chief of Police Hugh Brown informed us that no shots were fired.

In York, 11 persons were wounded in a "gun battle" on the first night. However, it turns out that 10 out of 11 persons were civilians and were injured by shotgun pellets. Only two snipers were involved, and only two to four shots were fired throughout the entire disturbance.

In Waterloo, Iowa, Chief of Police Robert S. Wright acknowledged that shots were fired, but he added: "We wouldn't consider it sniper fire." He told us that there was "no ambush, no concealment of participants, or anything like that." Moreover, he stated that not more than three persons out of a crowd of 50 youths carried weapons and "not a great number of shots were fired." The weapons used were small handguns.

In St. Paul, where 10 shots were reportedly fired at police and four officers were wounded by gunshots, Chief of Police Lester McAuliffe also acknowledged that though there was gunfire, there "wasn't any sniper fire as such."

A similar situation was found in Peoria. Safety Director Kennedy said that the three shots believed fired did not constitute actual sniping.

In Little Rock, Chief Brians discounted reports of widespread sniping and indicated that many "shots" were really firecrackers.

In Gary, early reports were that Chief of Police James Hilton had been fired upon and six persons had been wounded by snipers. Assistant Chief of Police Charles Boone told us that while a few shots might have been "fired in the air," no actual sniping occurred. No one was shot during the disturbance, and no one was injured. Chief Hilton indicated that the fireman who was supposed to have been hit during the outbreak was actually shot by a drunk *prior* to the disorder.

In a few instances, discrepancies between first reports and sober reappraisal can be traced to exaggerations of the policemen themselves. However, most of the discrepancies already cited throughout this report can be attributed to the press—at both the local and national level. In some instances, the early press reports (those appearing at the time of the incident) were so inexplicit as to give the *impression* of a great deal of sniping. In other instances, the early figures given were simply exaggerated. In still other instances, the early reports failed to distinguish between sniper fire and other forms of gunplay.

Moreover, the press generally gave far too little attention to the immediate cause or causes of the disturbance. Even in the aftermath of the violence, few attempts were made to verify previous statements or to survey the tensions and grievances rooted in the community. Instead, newspapers in many instances placed an unusually heavy (and at times distorted) emphasis on the most dramatic aspects of the violence, particularly where sniping was concerned.

A look at some of the newspaper headlines during the disorders is most revealing, especially where the "pellet cases" are involved. As mentioned earlier, large numbers of casualties were sustained from the pellets of a single shotgun blast—in Peoria, seven policemen; in Harvey-Dixmoor, five policemen, and in York, 10 civilians were injured in this way; the most commonly cited examples of a "new pattern" of violence. Unfortunately, inaccurate and sensational headlines created an impression of widespread sniping, with the police singled out as the principal targets. A few individual acts of violence were so enlarged as to convey to the reader a series of "bloodbaths." In some cases, an explanation of the circumstances surrounding the injuries was buried in the news story. In other cases, no explanation was given. In still other cases, the number of casualties was exaggerated.

Distorted headlines were found in the local press:

RACE VIOLENCE ERUPTS: DOZEN SHOT IN PEORIA
Chicago (Ill.) *Tribune,*
July 31, 1968

6 COPS ARE SHOT IN HARVEY STRIFE
Chicago *Sun-Times,*
August 7, 1968

20 HURT AS NEW VIOLENCE RAKES WEST END AREA
11 FELLED BY GUN FIRE, FOUR FIREMEN INJURED FIGHTING FIVE
BLAZES
York (Pa.) *Dispatch,*
August 5, 1968

These distortions were transmitted on the wire services as well. For example, in Ann Arbor, Michigan, readers were given the following accounts of Peoria and Harvey-Dixmoor in their local newspapers. The first account was based upon a United Press International news dispatch; the second is from an Associated Press dispatch.

10 POLICEMEN SHOT IN PEORIA VIOLENCE

By United Press International
Ann Arbor (Mich.) *News,*
July 30, 1968

Ten policemen were wounded by shotgun blasts today during a four-hour flareup of violence in Peoria, Ill. . . .

EIGHT WOUNDED IN CHICAGO AREA

Ann Arbor *News,*
August 7, 1968

Harvey, Ill. (AP)—Sporadic gunfire wounded seven policemen and a woman during a disturbance caused by Negro youths, and scores of law enforcement officers moved in early today to secure the troubled area. . . .

Finally, they were repeated in headlines and stories appearing in the national press:

GUNFIRE HITS 11 POLICEMEN IN ILL. VIOLENCE

Washington Post,
July 31, 1968

SHOTGUN ASSAULTS IN PEORIA GHETTO WOUND 9 POLICEMEN

The Law Officer,
Fall, 1968

Chicago—On August 6, in the suburbs of Harvey and Dixmoor, seven policemen and a woman were shot in Negro disturbances which a Cook County undersheriff said bore signs of having been planned.

U.S. News & World Report
August 19, 1968

In all probability, few newspapers or reporters could withstand this type of criticism. Nevertheless, it does seem that the national press bears a special responsibility. Few of the nationally known newspapers and magazines attempted to verify sniping reports coming out of the cities; few were willing to undertake independent investigations of their own; and far too many were overly zealous in their reports of a "trend" based on limited and unconfirmed evidence. Stated very simply: The national press overreacted.

For some time now, many observers (including members of the academic community) have been predicting a change from spontaneous to premeditated outbreaks resembling guerrilla warfare. Their predictions have largely been based upon limited evidence such as unconfirmed reports of arms caches and the defiant, sometimes revolutionary rhetoric of militants.

And then came Cleveland. At the time, the July disorder in that city appeared to fulfill all the predictions—intelligence reports of planning prior to the disorder, intensive sniping directed at the police, the absence of a precipitating incident, and so on. Few people at the time quarreled with the appraisal in *The New York Times* that Cleveland was "perhaps the first documented case" of a planned uprising against the police. Following the events in Cleveland, disorders in which shots may have been fired were immediately suspected to be part of a "wave."

Unwittingly or not, the press has been constructing a scenario on armed uprisings. The story line of this scenario is not totally removed from reality. There *have* been a few shoot-outs with the police, and a handful may have been planned. But no wave of uprisings and no set pattern of murderous conflict have developed—at least not yet. Has the press provided the script for future conspiracies? Why hasn't the scenario been acted out until now? The answers to these questions are by no means certain. What is clear is that the press has critical responsibilities in this area, for any act of violence easily attracts the attention of the vicarious viewer as well as the participant.

Moreover, in an era when most Americans are informed by radio and television, the press should place far greater emphasis on interpreting, rather than merely reporting, the news. Background pieces on the precipitating events and tension-heightening incidents, more detailed information on the sniper himself, and investigations concerning police and civilian casualties represent fertile areas for the news analyst. To close, here is one concrete example: While four policemen were killed in the violence reviewed in this article, at least 16 civilians were also killed. A report on the circumstances of these deaths might provide some important insights into the disorders.

July / August 1969

FURTHER READING SUGGESTED BY THE AUTHOR:

The Paranoid Style in American Politics and Other Essays by Richard Hofstadter (New York: Knopf, 1966). A historian looks at the receptiveness of Americans to conspiratorial theories.

Shoot-out in Cleveland; Black Militants and the Police: July 23, 1968. A report of the Civil Violence Research Center by Louis H. Masotti and James J. Corsi (Cleveland, Ohio: Case Western Reserve University, submitted to the National Commission on the Causes and Prevention of Violence, May 16, 1969). This is an in-depth account of the background, nature, and circumstances of the July, 1968 disorder.

Public Information and Civil Disorders, National League of Cities, Department of Urban Studies (Washington, D.C.: July, 1968) contains recommendations concerning the activities of the news media during civil disorders.

Report of the National Advisory Commission on Civil Disorders (Washington, D.C.: Government Publishing Office, 1968). Chapter 15 evaluates the media coverage of civil disorders during the Summer of 1967.

Confrontation
At Cornell

WILLIAM H. FRIEDLAND/HARRY EDWARDS

Bandoliers across their shoulders, rifles and shotguns casually held ready, the black students of Cornell broke into American consciousness one morning last April like an advance patrol of that army of barbarians which is the special nightmare of the affluent and, for some, their dream of regeneration. In that moment, fear—which everyone on the campus, both black and white, had known for days—rippled out and touched everyone.

Cornell seems an unlikely, not to say preposterous setting for such an event. Tucked away in rural upstate New York, the college until recently was comfortably settled in an atmosphere of genteel WASPishness. There was also an Ivy League rah-rah spirit about the place which only partially obscured the substantial number of lower-class youths who came to Ithaca under State University auspices to study agriculture, education and home economics. True, there had been a riot in 1958 (memorialized in Richard Farina's novel *Been Down So Long It Looks Like Up to Me*) over the right of students to have mixed parties without chaperons. But *political* activism came late to Cornell.

The trigger was pulled at Berkeley in 1964. After that, Cornell students began to organize themselves, somewhat feebly, into a group called Students For Education. SFE, before being washed away by the Vietnam escalation of 1965, brought into being a good many study commissions and some small changes, among them the conversion of the campus bookstore into a bookstore rather than a purveyor of required texts, setting up an on-campus coffee house, and some very limited changes in the grading system.

But as the Vietnam war went on and was intensified, students at Cornell, like those elsewhere, stepped up their protests. One major confrontation took place during an ROTC review in the college's cavernous Barton Hall, which later figured so importantly in the events of the Spring. Throughout this period, most student activism revolved around the Students for a Democratic Society. Like SDS everywhere, the Cornell group was anti-organizational, anti-leadership, using consensus decision-making procedures, committed to spontaneity. Despite this (or because of it), SDS has been remarkably efficient in mobilizing on the part of the students and a few faculty members.

Until recently, the number of blacks at Cornell has been negligible. Indeed, into the early 1960's, those from outside the United States were far more numerous than American blacks. Furthermore, as at most American universities, the atmosphere at Cornell was almost unashamedly racist. Many fraternities, for example, constitutionally denied membership to non-Caucasians. But as the civil rights movement gathered force in the country, Cornell's liberals began to put pressure on the restrictive practices of the fraternities and tried to eliminate discrimination in off-campus housing. And Cornell students were among those who participated in the Freedom Summer of 1964, working on voter registration in Fayette County, Tennessee.

White involvement in civil rights activities fell off in 1965 however. The development of racial consciousness among blacks led to the belief that blacks had to make their own way and shed themselves of their white supporters if their movement was to be their own. Then, too, the escalation of the Vietnam war increasingly provided a focus for liberal and radical whites. At the same time, more significant changes were taking place at Cornell as the number of American black students began to increase. A Committee on Special Educational Projects (COSEP) was set up to locate and recruit black students and provide them with financial and other support. COSEP's success, while small, was such that by September 1968 there were 240 blacks at Cornell in a total of some 13,200.

But even before then, the presence of black students was causing considerable strain in the university. The separatist issue broke into the open when a black girl, living in the girls' dorms, experienced difficulties with her dormmates. The girl was referred to Cornell's clinic for psychiatric assistance and apparently found little sympathy there. Ordered to leave Cornell, she refused. This precipitated a crisis out of which came demands for separate housing so that blacks could be free of the pressures of living in a hostile environment. Reluctantly, the college made arrangements to establish several black co-ops.

Later, academic freedom seemed to many to be called into question when black students and others became convinced that a visiting professor was teaching racism. After complaining to every relevant agency of the university and being put off time after time, the blacks confronted the professor with the demand that he read a statement in class. When he insisted on reading it in advance and the blacks rejected this, he dismissed the class. The blacks thereupon sat in at the professor's department offices, holding the department chairman in his office.

On that same day occurred the assassination of Martin Luther King and the two events provided the university community with a rarely experienced shock. In addition, several fires were set and later, blacks used Cornell's memorial service to King as an opportunity to attack the university and America's whites.

If nothing else, these events during the year 1967-68 indicated that the blacks at Cornell had layed a strong base for their organization which soon everyone would know as the Afro-American Society.

In response to events of the 1968 spring term, the university moved to set up an Afro-American studies program. Throughout the summer and fall a committee made up of nine faculty and administration members and eight black students met to work out the program. But in the second week of December the black students revolted against what they saw as stalling tactics. They demanded total control of the program and refused to cooperate any further with the existing committee. The same week, six members of the Afro-American Society forced three whites to leave their offices in a university building on Waite Avenue—a building that the administration had promised to the Afro-American studies program, and during the same affair a photographer for the *Cornell Daily Sun* was roughed up when he refused to turn over a film.

At the same time, however, covert negotiations between the black students and the administration continued over the demands for an autonomous black studies program, but little progress was made and the blacks saw this as another expression of Cornell's unwillingness to take their demands seriously. Consequently, one week before the Christmas recess, black students at Cornell staged a number of demonstrations. Groups of them marched around the quadrangles playing bongo drums, while another contingent entered the President's office with water pistols. They also pushed white students away from several tables in the student union and claimed them for themselves as "black tables." Another time, they carried hundreds of books from the library shelves to the checkout counters, and dumped them there as "irrelevant." They also went to the clinic and demanded treatment by a black physician. Despite their sometimes playful aspects, these demonstrations had an ugly and threatening undercurrent that left most whites tense. Nevertheless, the administration did move toward implementing a black studies program. Not all black demands were met, but a black was chosen to be acting director and compromises were worked out that made the program a degree-granting one. Another consequence was that the black students saw their demonstrations as part of a political program necessary to help them gain a meaningful education at Cornell.

Still, the faculty and administration response to the demonstrations had been hostile and the process of finding scapegoats upon whom retribution might be visited got underway. In January, six students were charged before the Student-Faculty Conduct Board. The decision with respect to these students was one of the important factors leading to the 1969 confrontation.

The disciplinary issues were complicated by what happened during a conference on apartheid sponsored by Cornell's Center for International Studies. The 25 speakers, of whom only three were black, were not greeted sympathetically by an audience composed for the most part of Afro-Americans, black Africans, and SDS supporters. The latter moved rapidly from verbal hostility to more openly disruptive interventions. At a meeting on the second evening of the conference, the blacks turned out en masse to challenge Cornell President James Perkins on university investments in South Africa. As Perkins was speaking, one black student grabbed him by the collar and pulled him from the podium. Perkins, badly shaken, left the room. The campus reaction to this incident was hardly in favor of the blacks, despite the fact that there was an increasing sentiment that Cornell's endowments should be free of the taint of apartheid.

Meanwhile, preliminary to the trial of the six members of the Afro-American Society before the Student-Faculty Conduct Board, the AAS was claiming that the demonstrations of December had been political acts for which the organization should be held responsible. Selection of a few members could only be regarded as victimization. Accordingly, the six refused to appear before the Conduct Board. Then followed a period in which the six students were verbally threatened with suspension if they failed to appear before the Board. When they didn't show up, letters were sent. In April, just before the events that brought Cornell into the headlines, an obscure clause was discovered that permitted the Conduct Board to take action without the black students being present. On April 18, the Conduct Board reprimanded three of the blacks, dismissed charges against two others, while the charge against the last student was dropped because of his departure from the university.

Throughout this period, campus groups had been enunciating principles to support their positions on the issues involved. For the Conduct Board (and implicitly for the faculty and much of the student body) the issue raised was: Is the university a single community? If it is *a* community, must all "citizens" adhere to its rules? The blacks not only challenged the idea of *a* community but put forward the principle that no man should be judged except by a jury of his peers. The blacks also challenged the legitimacy of the Board, contending it was not a voluntary product of the campus community but one imposed by the racist apparatus of American society. In partial justification of their statement, the Afro-Americans pointed out that there was no black representation on the Board. A second conflict of principle arose over the issue of how personal, in contrast to political, acts could be judged. Some university groups argued that individuals rather than organizations had to be held responsible for their acts; organizations could not be tried before the Conduct Board. The blacks asserted the reverse was true: their actions were political, therefore their responsibility was collective. The blacks also argued that the university was not only the aggrieved party but the judge and jury as well, and principles of Anglo-Saxon justice declared that this should not be done. The Afro-American Society suggested that "arbitration" as in industrial-relations might be the appropriate model for a resolution of the problem.

In addition to the disciplinary issue, a number of other questions were deeply troubling to numbers of both students and faculty. During their seizure of the Waite Avenue building the blacks had insisted that their demands for an Afro-American studies program were "nonnegotiable." This was pure rhetoric, negotiations were going on through intermediaries, and most people knew it. Nevertheless, many faculty members interpreted the position of the blacks as needlessly intransigent. The black separatism issue had not gone down well with much of the university community either, especially those tables in the student union which had been claimed as black territory. Blacks moved around the campus in groups and were never found fraternizing with whites. This was upsetting to most faculty and students.

While attention centered on the blacks during the spring, a host of other issues affected large numbers of white students. sds had made demands that the university provide housing not only for students but for the Ithaca community. Arguing that Cornell had thrown the burden of housing upon the community, sds insisted that the university provide low-cost housing units for underprivileged groups in Ithaca. This issue generated considerable support in faculty and student circles: a network of housing organizations was created to bring pressures for a university commitment. A second issue burgeoned over the impending departure of several noted historians and humanities professors. Humanities has not been strong at Cornell; it is not an area to which the administration has paid any serious attention. So the issue was one that mobilized many Arts and Sciences students. Still other grievances were those of graduate assistants over financial support, and Cornell's South African investments. And, in mid-April, just before the confrontation, a popular sociology professor, one of the first winners of a teaching award, was refused tenure because of his weak publication record.

These issues, and others, created an atmosphere of tension that threatened to come to a crisis on Wednesday, March 12, when the university faculty was scheduled to meet. But when the day came, the faculty adopted a resolution supporting the integrity of the adjudicatory machinery of the Conduct Board and the situation continued to bubble with neither confrontation nor resolution.

At 3:00 A.M. on the morning of Friday, April 18, persons still unknown threw a burning cross on the porch of the black girls' co-operative. Responding to a call, the campus safety patrol reached the co-op where the fire was stamped out. What exactly the campus safety patrol did at the scene of the cross-burning is not clear, but apparently all seven officers covering the incident withdrew, ostensibly on other business, leaving no protection at the co-op. Much later, a guard was established, but by that time the blacks had evidently lost any confidence they may have had in campus protection. This was to be exacerbated as campus officials, while strongly deploring the incident, referred to it as a "thoughtless prank." To the blacks, the symbolism of the event was as powerful as if someone had burned a *Mogen David* in front of a Jewish fraternity. Had such a thing occurred, the blacks reasoned, all the powers of the university would have been brought to bear and the cries of outrage would have been mighty indeed. As it was, the somewhat cavalier attitudes of the university seemed still another reflection of institutional racism, less open perhaps than the occasional group of white boys who had shouted "nigger" at black girls, but racism it was, nevertheless.

As word of the cross-burning spread among the blacks, they assembled at the co-op to decide what action was necessary to protect their women. The defense of their own kind, this was to become a central symbol of the events that followed. As for their choice of target—the student union at Willard Straight Hall, this was in part dictated by the dramatic possibilities implicit in the fact that Parents' Weekend had begun and the opportunity to demonstrate before thousands of parents was tactically so tempting that rumors had been circulating that some group would seize some building somewhere regardless of the issue. How significant a role the rumors played in the deliberations of the blacks is not known, but the tactical impact of the seizure was clear. But it is clear that in deciding to take over the student union, the blacks were intent only on giving an emphatic warning to the campus to "get off our backs," they were not concerned with specific demands. Indeed, the original intent was to seize the building for one day only and then surrender it peaceably.

At 6:00 A.M. on Saturday, April 19, the blacks marched into Willard Straight Hall, calmly ordered service personnel preparing for the day's activities to remove themselves, expelled from guest rooms in the loft a number of visiting parents, and locked up the building.

News of the seizure soon spread throughout the campus; by 8:00 A.M. everyone knew the university was on the brink of another confrontation. For many of the students, particularly those at either end of the political spectrum, having an audience of parents probably served as a stimulus to action. The conservative students tend to be concentrated in a small number of houses that remain "lily-white" and in the fraternities. One of these, Delta Upsilon, is known as the "jock house," because of its unusual number of athletes. It is also one of the most WASPish houses and at present includes no Negro members. Around 9:00 in the morning, about 15 to 20 DU members attempted to break into Straight Hall, and some eight or nine succeeded in getting in before a group of SDS people prevented the rest from entering. While a good deal of pushing, shoving, and arguing was going on outside, inside there was a brief but violent battle between the blacks and the DU men. Three whites and one black were injured, no one seriously. The battle ended with the expulsion of the fraternity boys, but the blacks, even though badly shaken, announced that any other attack would be met by mounting escalation of force. SDS members, standing outside in sympathy with the blacks, rejected a proposal to seize another building and maintained a picket around the entire building to show their support.

The DU attack can be, and was, interpreted in various ways. But from the viewpoint of the blacks, it represented a university attempt to oust them from the building. The campus patrol was supposed to have been guarding the building to prevent entry. Therefore, the fact that the DU people had gotten in was all too easily understood by the blacks as administrative complicity, rather than what it probably was—a spontaneous, self-organized attempt by frat boys. For their part, the DU men insisted that they had entered the building to engage in discussion with black athletes inside and that there was no intent to recapture the building. (There is no evidence, however, that there were ever any black athletes involved in the seizure of the student union.) The DU men claimed that they went in empty-handed; the blacks insisted that they came in with clubs.

Following this incident, the campus gave itself up to an orgy of rumors. Throughout the day, it was circulated about that armed vigilante groups were preparing to mount an attack on Straight Hall. Inside the Hall, the blacks received continuous telephone messages about these vigilantes. By Saturday afternoon, according to the testimony of the blacks and the administrators in telephone contact with them, the occupiers were in a state of terrible tension. It was then that they decided to bring in guns to protect themselves. In the end, they were to have 13 rifles, and two shotguns.

Saturday night passed quietly, but the tension throughout the campus was approaching a critical point. By Sunday morning, Cornell administrators had decided that it would be necessary to end the occupation of the Straight at almost any cost.

That the occupation of the Straight was a precipitous act, probably triggered by the cross-burning, is attested to, first, by the lengthy time it took the blacks to formulate demands; and, second, the relatively flimsy nature of the demands. By Saturday afternoon, three had emerged from Willard Straight, of which one was subsequently withdrawn. The first demand called for a nullification of the three reprimands handed down by the Conduct Committee after the demonstrations of December; the second called for a full investigation and report of the Afro-American Society of the cross-burning incident. That the blacks would take such very serious steps for such tired and modest demands indicates their state of fear and tension. But this was never communicated to the campus, except to those in the administration, Dean Robert Miller especially, who were in direct contact with them. With the latter, the blacks entered into a six-point agreement to end the Straight occupation. It included a commitment to call a full faculty meeting and recommend that the reprimands be declared null and void.

However, the occupiers of Straight Hall were still determined to demonstrate to Cornell whites that they were no longer sitting ducks. So it was that despite pressure from administrators for a decorous exit, the blacks proceeded to make a dramatic exit, brandishing their weapons. It soon became convenient for the shocked white majority of the university to look upon this as a new escalation in student activism; while campus after campus had experienced confrontation, it was argued that this was the first time that students had taken up guns. It was within this context that Cornell arrived at a new level of internal tension on Monday, April 21.

The sight of armed students marching across their campus was too much for the overwhelming majority of the faculty. Unable to understand, or ignorant of, the black students' side of the story, their immediate reaction on

Monday, April 21, was one of bitter hostility to any compromise or accommodation of black demands. Their antagonism focused on the six-point agreement reached between the administration and the blacks. Some forty members of the faculty, largely in the government and history departments, signed a statement declaring they would resign if the reprimands were nullified at the Monday faculty meeting.

Tension increased during the day as the opposition to nullification crystallized in the faculty. What the reaction of the blacks would be to a refusal to nullify was unclear, but there was an unspoken and widespread fear that Cornell might be headed toward some kind of shoot-out. In these circumstances, President Perkins called a convocation in Barton Hall just before the university faculty meeting. Some 10,000 students, faculty and staff assembled to hear an innocuous 20-minute statement by the President that left issues more undefined than before. There had been an expectation that presidential leadership was to be asserted.

Instead, in an atmosphere of diffuse fear and anger, in which the focused hostility of the government and history departments stood out, the faculty assembled at 4:00 P.M. in unprecedented numbers. The meeting began with a report by Dean of the Faculty, Robert Miller, who introduced a formal motion calling for nullification of the reprimands. The Dean's assessment was that the danger to human life at Cornell was real and had to be avoided even at the cost of failing to sustain the authority of the adjudicatory machinery, the Conduct Board. This approach was rejected by the faculty. Instead, they voted a substitute motion that upheld the legitimacy of the adjudicatory machinery and took no action on the nullification of the reprimands. Continuing for over four hours of intricate parliamentary maneuvers, the faculty meeting showed that the majority was adamantly opposed to nullification, but there was also an obdurate, vocal minority supporting the blacks or concerned with the consequences of refusal to nullify. President Perkins had little political capital at this meeting despite his earlier proclamation of limited emergency, a statement that anyone carrying guns on university property would be suspended summarily, or that disruptive demonstrations would lead to immediate suspensions. Nevertheless, he was able to achieve minimal consensus with a resolution calling for the initiation of discussions between the Faculty Council and the Afro-American Society and calling for another full faculty meeting.

Dean Miller now tendered his resignation, stating that by the refusal to vote on his motion, the faculty was repudiating his estimate of the situation. He was promptly given a standing ovation, which neatly illustrated the faculty's dilemma. They respected him and wanted peace, but they felt they had to refuse to make concessions under what they saw as the threat of armed coercion. As the meeting ended at 8:15 and the faculty departed for long-delayed dinners, there was the sense that no solution had been found and that the campus was entering a new and more dangerous situation.

On Monday evening SDS called a meeting attended by 2,500, but it ended inconclusively. SDS was waiting for the blacks.

By Tuesday morning the campus was in chaos. Many classes did not meet, and in those that did the only topics were those raised by the confrontation. The university leadership, seeking desperately to remedy a deteriorating situation, consulted the deans of the colleges and proposed meetings of college faculties and the beginning of a broad-based discussion at all levels. The intent was to structure free-floating campus anxieties into organized meetings geared to a search for solutions. In the leadership vacuum created by the conflict between the administration's willingness to make concessions and an obdurate faculty, the administration sought only to keep a dialogue going. The fear of bloodshed was everywhere.

At noon, an ephemeral organization named "The Concerned Faculty," consisting largely of elements supporting the blacks, convened for several hours. Urged on by members of the Afro-American Society, "The Concerned Faculty" were unable to decide on anything more than gestures of solidarity. Twenty-six of those attending agreed to seize a building if necessary, while some 60-odd announced their willingness to strike.

Meanwhile, however, at meetings of the faculties of the various colleges, an apparent change in campus opinion began to be felt. The colleges of Arts and Sciences and Home Economics voted to recommend nullification of the Conduct Board's reprimands, and at its 7:00 P.M. meeting, the Faculty Council did the same, while calling for another meeting of the faculty for Wednesday noon. But several other faculties were still determined to maintain business as usual.

That same Tuesday, student opinion on campus began crystallizing around a call by SDS and the Inter-Fraternity Council for a teach-in at Barton Hall, the largest building on campus. By early evening, thousands of students had begun moving to the Hall. Like the faculty, they too seemed intent on avoiding violence between the blacks and other forces. Somewhere between 8,000 to 10,000 people gathered there and as the evening went on, a consensus emerged that it was vital for Cornell students to remain in the building and act as a pressure group on the Cornell faculty, which was scheduled to meet the next day, Wednesday, April 23. SDS speakers proposed that the students declare that they had seized the building, thereby defying President Perkins' new regulation prohibiting such actions. Only a handful objected, and later in the evening Perkins condoned the occupation of Barton Hall, though he persisted in defining it as a teach-in rather than as the seizure the students had declared it to be. This "legal" anomaly continued through the night. Thousands made preparations for the all-night meeting; a collection was taken and soon sandwiches and drinks were being passed out among the teeming mass of students.

As the evening of Tuesday, April 22 wore on, students organized according to their colleges to lobby faculty members for their vote on Wednesday. Around the edges of the Hall, there were dozens of meetings involving tens and hundreds of students. At 3:00 A.M. meetings were still continuing; they included not only groups from different colleges, but various ad hoc committees on the press, particularly the *Sun,* the university's student operated newspaper. One large group of biology students was attempting to deal with the problem of a professor who refused to cancel a quiz scheduled for the next day. The mood in Barton Hall was tensely hopeful; that such an incredible outpouring of students could take place showed that student sentiment had shifted to the blacks, although it was less clear whether the shift had occurred for substantive reasons or because of the fear of violence.

On Wednesday, April 23, the students were wakened by a banjo ensemble and the speech-making began again in the Hall. Elsewhere on the campus, hundreds of meetings were taking place as faculty member. were visited by student lobbyists.

Soon after the faculty meeting was gavelled into session by Provost Dale Corson, it became evident that a clear shift had occurred among the members. Despite hardline speeches by government and history faculty members, a motion to nullify was replaced by a second motion which not only called for nullification but also for restructuring the university. The substitute was introduced by Professor Clinton Rossiter who had signed, only two days before, the statement threatening resignation if the reprimands were nullified. Biology professor William Keaton explained how a large delegation of his students from Barton Hall had asked him to change his vote, not because of the threat of violence, but because they wanted him to have faith in them. But the probable major reason for the shift was expressed by Nobel physicist, Hans Bethe, who said that since the moderates were moving toward the SDS left, it was necessary for the faculty to reverse itself to occupy the middle ground and isolate radicals. The resolution calling for nullification and restructuring the university carried by a voice vote probably on the order of three or four to one. The faculty now accepted a resolution by philosopher Max Black informing the students "We hear you. . . ."

A thousand faculty members then moved to Barton Hall where they received a standing ovation. The faculty action demonstrated to the students the latter's influence on the decision-making process; from this point, emphasis shifted to the second part of the Rossiter resolution on restructuring the university.

As the faculty arrived, Eric Evans, vice president of the Afro-American Society was talking. President Perkins came to the podium where, according to Evans, he put his arm around him, smiled in fatherly fashion, and said "Sit down, I want to talk." Evans refused to surrender the microphone. Nothing better demonstrated the students' new mood than the hilarious cheering that broke out when Evans informed them of this exchange. While Perkins fidgeted uncomfortably on the floor with the students and faculty, Evans continued a leisurely review of events leading up to the Willard Straight seizure. When he finished, Perkins spoke and was followed by a succession of others. Slowly the Barton Hall meeting achieved a catharsis from the tensions of the past five days. By 5:00 P.M. the teach-in had ended. Cornell now entered a new phase ostensibly dedicated to a restructuring of the university.

The period immediately following the Barton Hall catharsis was characterized by what can only be called organizational withdrawal symptoms. The most dramatic occurred within SDS which either could not or would not come to grips with its lack of organization and need for leadership. The faculty, too, lost the capacity to function coherently as a corporate body. The Afro-Americans managed to rename themselves the Black Liberation Front but otherwise they also retreated into themselves to try to decide how to relate to the college community under the new circumstances.

Administration officials and traditionally apathetic students also withdrew. The administration was in a state of shock; all that emerged from Day Hall, the administration building, were generalized statements reinforcing previous statements about guns and disruptive demonstrations. Beyond that, Day Hall demonstrated no capacity to provide any structure, guidance, or direction. As for the students, once catharsis had been achieved on Wednesday they lost the capacity to act.

In these circumstances, the tendency was to revert to the traditional, though weakened, institutional structure. Students and faculty turned to colleges and departments, that is, to more manageable social units. With this, the cooling-off process began. It was not that everyone's behavior was as in the past, but students once again came into direct face-to-face relations with teachers, to whom they had always exhibited deference. In a (crude) word, the "reniggerization" of the students had begun.

But the cooling-off took time. It was a week before student statements became more qualified and less concrete and hard-line. Faculty statements, too, became tougher as the teachers reverted to traditional issues of teaching vs. research, academic freedom, and the like.

What this means is that any action with respect to change in university structure, functioning, and priorities will be based on traditional university norms and values. Moreover, the summer will be used as a cooling-off period. Once again there will be the gradual accretion of "data," the rational consideration of infinitesimal details. This does not mean that the faculty will be unwilling to change at all; rather that change will be oriented toward maintaining basic structures. Cooptation of student dissidents will become the major mechanicism for attempting to alleviate pressure, for it is evident that the major emphasis is now on alleviating pressure, not solving problems. More fundamental commitment to change in the governance of the university or the educational process remains small.

In the weeks following the adjournment of Barton Hall, the administration, the students, and the faculty have been inadvertently laying the foundation for the next confrontation by reversion to old structures.

But first, it is perhaps worth a short digression to examine why so few black students at Cornell have been able to create such enormous pressures (and we limit ourselves to Cornell here, although some of this analysis is appropriate to black-student experience at other universities).

There is, first of all, a reservoir of readily exploitable guilt in liberal academic circles, but much more depends upon the social situation of a relatively small number of blacks resident in an overwhelmingly white university. All students experience adaptation and living problems in residential universities. Thrown together for long periods of intensive community living and having to navigate a host of curricular and extracurricular problems and opportunities, most students have to find ways of making it all manageable.

As blacks increased at Cornell they experienced the usual problems that blacks undergo in a white environment. But the present generation of black collegians entered the university just as black-power ideology began to affect black intellectuals. This, and the antipathy they felt on the part of the whites, led black students into closer and more intensive relations with each other. The coalescence was further intensified by such incidents as that of whites yelling "nigger" at black girls. Each incident was stored away and became the subject of continual discussion. In these circumstances, black students began to act against their environment and their number was exactly right for the maximum cohesiveness needed to generate pressures. If larger number of blacks were present, this cohesiveness would be difficult, if not impossible.

But the main grounds on which we would predict further troubles for Cornell are the discrepancies between student hopes for change and the structural inabilities of universities to obtain significant change, especially in the educational process. This will create serious problems because the demand of students for restructuring the learning process remains unresolved. At the same time, the social conditions contributing to this demand also remain unresolved: poverty, discrimination, racism, the war in Vietnam, continue and are interpreted, probably correctly, as worsening. Most students are naive in that they think university reform will take place by itself, and many believe that something tangible will come out of Barton Hall. As students realize that little or nothing can emerge, they will find themselves increasingly frustrated.

The specific issue that will trigger the next action can come from a variety of sources: recruitment by employers (which most universities will not eliminate because a majority of students want it), pressures for open recruitment of blacks or other deprivileged groups, financial shortages as alumni react against campus actions, relations with the surrounding community, university investments, and so on. Thus, the institutional inabilities to change rapidly and drastically practically guarantee new confrontations in the next academic year at Cornell.

June 1969

The Making
Of the Negro Mayors,
1967

JEFFREY K. HADDEN/LOUIS H. MASOTTI
VICTOR THIESSEN

Throughout most of 1967, black power and Vietnam kept this nation in an almost continual state of crisis. The summer months were the longest and hottest in modern U.S. history—many political analysts even felt that the nation was entering its most serious domestic conflict since the Civil War. Over a hundred cities were rocked with violence.

As the summer gave way to autumn, the interest of the nation shifted a little from the summer's riots to the elections on the first Tuesday of November. An unprecedented number of Negroes were running for office, but public attention focused on three elections. In Cleveland, Carl B. Stokes, a lawyer who in 1962 had become the first Democratic Negro legislator in Ohio, was now seeking to become the first Negro mayor of a large American city. In Gary, Ind., another young Negro lawyer, Richard D. Hatcher, was battling the Republican Party's candidate—as well as his own Democratic Party—to become the first Negro mayor of a "medium-sized" city. And in Boston, Louise Day Hicks, a symbol of white backlash, was conducting a "You know where I stand" campaign to capture the mayorality.

Normally, the nation couldn't care less about who would become the next mayors of Cleveland, Gary, and Boston. But the tenseness of the summer months gave these elections enormous significance. If Stokes and Hatcher lost and Hicks won, could Negroes be persuaded to use the power of the ballot box rather than the power of fire bombs?

Fortunately, November 7 proved to be a triumphant day for racial peace. Stokes and Hatcher won squeaker victories, both by margins of only about 1500 votes; in Boston, Kevin H. White defeated Mrs. Hicks by a 12,000 plurality. Labor leader George Meany was exultant—"American voters have rejected racism as a political issue." Negroes in the three cities were also jubilant. In Gary, the most tense of the cities, Richard Hatcher urged the mostly Negro crowd at his head-quarters to "cool it." "I urge that the outcome of this election be unmarred by any incident of any kind. . . . If we spoil this victory with any kind of occur-rence here tonight, or anywhere in the city, it will be a hollow victory." The evening *was* cool: Joyous Negroes danced and sang in the streets.

But beyond the exultation of victory remain many hard questions. Now that Cleveland and Gary have Negro mayors, just how much difference will it make in solving the many grave problems that these cities face? Will these victories cool militancy in urban ghettos next summer, or will the momentum of frus-

tration prove too great to put on the brakes? A careful analysis of *how* these candidates won office may
help provide the answers.

The focus of this report is on Cleveland because:

■ As residents of Cleveland, we are more familiar
with the campaign and the election.

■ Cleveland is unique because, in 1965, it had a special census. By matching voting wards with census
tracts, we can draw a clearer picture of voting behavior
than we could in the other cities, where rapid neighborhood transitions have made 1960 census data quite
unreliable in assessing voting patterns. Having examined Cleveland in some detail, we will draw some
comparisons with the Gary and Boston elections, then
speculate about their significance and implications.

Cleveland has something less than 2,000,000 residents. Among metropolitan areas in America, it ranks
eleventh in size. Like many other American cities, the
central city of Cleveland is experiencing an absolute decline in population—residents are fleeing from the
decaying core to the surrounding suburbs. The city
certainly ranks high both in terms of absolute and
proportional decline in the central-city population.

Between 1950 and 1960, the population of the
central city declined from 914,808 to 876,050, a loss
of almost 39,000. By 1965 the population had sunk
to 810,858, an additional loss of 65,000. But these
figures are only a partial reflection of the changing
composition of the population, since new Negro residents coming into the central city helped offset the
white exodus. *Between 1950 and 1960, nearly 142,000
white residents left the central city, and an additional
94,000 left between 1960 and 1965—nearly a quarter*

of a million in just 15 years.

During the same period the number of Negro residents of Cleveland rose from 147,847 to 279,352—an increase from 16.1 percent to 34.4 percent of the city's population. There is no evidence that this dramatic population redistribution has changed since the special 1965 census. Some suburbanization of Negroes is beginning on the east and southeast side of the city, but the pace is not nearly so dramatic as for whites. In 1960, approximately 97 percent of the Negroes in the metropolitan area lived in the central city. This percentage has probably declined somewhat since then—16,000 Negro residents have moved to East Cleveland. But the basic pattern of segregation in the metropolitan area remains. The development in East Cleveland is little more than an eastward extension of the ghetto, and the older, decaying residential units the Negroes have moved to are hardly "suburban" in character.

While the population composition of Cleveland is changing rapidly, whites are still a significant majority—about 62 percent. Again like many other central cities, a significant percentage of the white population comprises nationality groups that live in segregated sections, with a strong sense of ethnic identity and a deep fear of Negro encroachment. (In 1964, the bussing of Negro students into Murray Hill, an Italian neighborhood, resulted in rioting.)

In 1960, the census classified 43 percent of the central city's white residents as "foreign stock." In that year, five groups—Germans, Poles, Czechs, Hungarians, and Italians—had populations of 25,000 or greater; at least 20 other nationality groups were large enough to have to be contended with in the political arena. But today these ethnic groups—although unwilling to admit it—have become less than the controlling majority they constituted before 1960.

The Cuyahoga River divides Cleveland, physically as well as socially. When Negroes first began to move into the city, during World War I, they occupied the decaying section to the south and east of the central business district. As their numbers grew, they continued pushing in this direction and now occupy the larger part of the eastside (except for some ethnic strongholds). There are no stable, integrated neighborhoods in the central city—only areas in transition from white to black. To the west, the Cuyahoga River constitutes a barrier to Negro penetration.

Ever since 1941, when Frank Lausche was elected, Cleveland has had a succession of basically honest but unimaginative Democratic mayors. These mayors have kept their hold on City Hall by means of a relatively weak coalition of nationality groups. At no point in this 26-year Lausche dynasty did a mayor gather enough power to seriously confront the long-range needs and problems of the city.

By early 1967, the city had seemingly hit rock bottom. A long procession of reporters began arriving to write about its many problems. The racial unrest of the past several years had, during the summer of 1966, culminated in the worst rioting in Cleveland's history. This unrest was continuing to grow as several militant groups were organizing. Urban renewal was a dismal failure; in January, the Department of Housing and Urban Development even cut off the city's urban-renewal funds, the first such action by the Federal Government. The exodus of whites, along with business, shoved the city to the brink of financial disaster. In February, the Moody Bond Survey reduced the city's credit rating. In May, the Federal Government cut off several million dollars of construction funds—because the construction industry had failed to assure equal job opportunities for minority groups. In short, the city was, and remains, in deep trouble. And while most ethnic groups probably continued to believe that Cleveland was the "Best Location in the Nation," the Negro community—and a growing number of whites—were beginning to feel that Cleveland was the "Mistake on the Lake," and that it was time for a change.

Carl Stokes's campaign for mayor was his second try. In 1965, while serving in the state House of Representatives, he came within 2100 votes of defeating Mayor Ralph S. Locher. Stokes had taken advantage of a city-charter provision that lets a candidate file as an independent, and bypass the partisan primaries. Ralph McAllister, then president of the Cleveland School Board, did the same. For his hard line on *de facto* school segregation, however, McAllister had earned the enmity of the Negro community. The Republican candidate was Ralph Perk, the first Republican elected to a county-wide position (auditor) in many years. A second generation Czech-Bohemian, Perk hoped to win by combining his ethnic appeal with his program for the city (Perk's Plan). He had no opposition for his party's nomination. The fourth candidate was Mayor Locher, who had defeated Mark McElroy, county recorder and perennial candidate for something, in the Democratic primary.

It was in the 1965 Democratic primary that the first signs of a "black bloc" vote emerged. The Negroes, who had previously supported incumbent Democratic mayoral candidates, if not enthusiastically at least consistently, made a concerted effort to dump Locher in favor of McElroy. There were two reasons.

■ Locher had supported his police chief after the latter had made some tactless remarks about Negroes. Incensed Negro leaders demanded an audience with the mayor, and when he refused, his office was the scene of demonstrations, sit-ins, and arrests. At that point, as one of the local reporters put it, "Ralph Locher became a dirty name in the ghetto."

■ Stokes, as an independent, and his supporters hoped that the Democratic primary would eliminate the *stronger* candidate, Locher. For then a black bloc would have a good chance of deciding the general election because of an even split in the white vote.

Despite the Negro community's efforts, Locher won the primary and went on to narrowly defeat Stokes. Locher received 37 percent of the vote, Stokes 36 percent, Perk 17 percent, and McAllister 9 percent. Some observers reported that a last-minute whispering campaign in Republican precincts—to the effect that "A vote for Perk is a vote for Stokes"—may have given Locher enough Republican votes to win. The evidence: The popular Perk received only a 17 percent vote in a city where a Republican could be expected something closer to 25 percent. Had Perk gotten anything close to 25 percent, Stokes would have probably been elected two years earlier.

Although he made a strong showing in defeat, Carl Stokes's political future looked bleak. No one expected the Democratic leaders to give Stokes another opportunity to win by means of a split vote. Nor were there other desirable elected offices Stokes could seek. Cleveland has no Negro Congressman—largely because the heavy Negro concentration in the city has been "conveniently" gerrymandered. The only district where Stokes might have had a chance has been represented by Charles Vanik, a popular and liberal white, and as long as Vanik remained in Congress Stokes was locked out. Stokes's state Senate district was predominantly white; and a county or state office seemed politically unrealistic because of his race. So, in 1966, Stokes sought re-election to the state House unopposed.

Between 1965 and 1967, Cleveland went from bad to worse, physically, socially, and financially. With no other immediate possibilities, Stokes began to think about running for mayor again. The big question was whether to risk taking on Locher in the primary—or to file as an independent again.

In effect, Stokes s decision was made for him. Seth Taft, slated to be the Republican candidate, told Stokes he would withdraw from the election entirely if Stokes filed as an independent in order to gain the advantage of a three-man general election. Taft had concluded that his best strategy was to face a Negro, *alone,* or a faltering incumbent, *alone,* in the general election. But not both. In a three-man race with Locher and Stokes, Taft correctly assumed that he would be the man in the middle with no chance for victory. (Taft would have preferred to run as an independent—to gain Democratic votes—but the county Republican leader threatened to file *another* Republican candidate unless Taft ran as a Republican.)

Meanwhile, Locher committed blunder after blunder—and Democratic party leaders began to question whether he could actually win another election. In the weeks before filing for the primary, Democratic leaders even pressured Locher to accept a Federal judgeship and clear the way for the president of the city council to run. But the Democratic leaders in Cleveland are not noted for their strength or effectiveness, as is evidenced by the fact that none of the Democratic mayors since 1941 were endorsed by the party when they were first elected. When Locher refused to withdraw, the party reluctantly rallied behind him.

Another Democratic candidate was Frank P. Celeste, former mayor of the Republican westside suburb of Lakewood. Celeste established residency in the city, announced his candidacy early, and—despite pressure from the Democratic Party—remained in the primary race.

There was always the possibility that Celeste would withdraw from the primary, which would leave Stokes facing Locher alone. But the threat of Taft's withdrawal from the general election left Stokes with little choice but to face Locher head-on in the primary. A primary race against Locher and a strong Democrat was more appealing than a general election against Locher and a weak Republican.

Now, in 1965 Stokes had received only about 6000 white votes in the city in a 239,000 voter turnout. To win in the primary, he had to enlarge and consolidate the Negro vote—and increase his white support on the westside and in the eastside ethnic wards.

The first part of his strategy was a massive voter-registration drive in the Negro wards—to reinstate the potential Stokes voters dropped from the rolls for failing to vote since the 1964 Presidential election. The Stokes organization—aided by Martin Luther King Jr. and the Southern Christian Leadership Conference, as well as by a grant (in part earmarked for voter

TABLE I

| | City Totals | | | Negro Wards | | |
	1965 General	1967 Primary	1967 General	1965 General	1967 Primary	1967 General
Registered Voters	337,803	326,003	326,003	103,123	99,885	99,885
Turnout	239,479	210,926	257,157	74,396	73,360	79,591
% Turnout	70.9	64.7	78.9	72.1	73.4	79.7
Stokes Votes	85,716	110,769	129,829	63,550	70,575	75,586
% Stokes Votes	35.8	52.5	50.5	85.4	96.2	95.0

| | White Wards | | | Mixed Wards | | |
	1965 General	1967 Primary	1967 General	1965 General	1967 Primary	1967 General
Registered Voters	159,419	152,737	152,737	75,261	73,421	73,421
Turnout	111,129	88,525	119,883	53,962	49,105	57,113
% Turnout	69.7	58.0	78.5	71.7	66.9	77.8
Stokes Votes	3,300	13,495	23,158	18,866	26,699	30,872
% Stokes Votes	3.0	15.2	19.3	35.0	54.4	54.1

registration) from the Ford Foundation to the Cleveland chapter of CORE—did succeed in registering many Negroes. But there was a similar drive mounted by the Democratic Party on behalf of Locher. (Registration figures are not available by race.)

The second part of the Stokes strategy took him across the polluted Cuyahoga River into the white wards that had given him a mere 3 percent of the vote in 1965. He spoke wherever he would be received —to small groups in private homes, in churches, and in public and private halls. While he was not always received enthusiastically, he did not confront many hostile crowds. He faced the race issue squarely and encouraged his audience to judge him on his ability.

Stokes's campaign received a big boost when the *Plain Dealer,* the largest daily in Ohio, endorsed him. Next, the *Cleveland Press* called for a change in City Hall, but declined to endorse either Stokes or Celeste. But since the polls indicated that Celeste was doing very badly, this amounted to an endorsement of Stokes.

More people voted in this primary than in any other in Cleveland's history. When the ballots were counted, Stokes had 52.5 percent of the votes—he had defeated Locher by a plurality of 18,000 votes. Celeste was the man in the middle, getting only 4 percent of the votes, the lowest of any mayoral candidate in recent Cleveland history.

What produced Stokes's clear victory? Table I (above) reveals the answer. The decisive factor was the size of the Negro turnout. While Negroes constituted only about 40 percent of the voters, 73.4 percent of them turned out, compared with only 58.4 percent of the whites. Predominantly Negro wards cast 96.2 percent of their votes for Stokes. (Actually this figure underrepresents the Negro vote for Stokes, since some of the non-Stokes votes in these wards were cast by whites. Similarly, the 15.4 percent vote for Stokes in the predominantly white wards slightly overestimates the white vote because of the Negro minority.)

Newspaper and magazine reports of the primary election proclaimed that Stokes could not have won without the white vote. Our own estimate—based on matching wards with census tracts, and allowing for only slight shifts in racial composition in some wards since the 1965 special census—is that Stokes received 16,000 white votes. His margin of victory was 18,000. How would the voting have gone if the third man, Celeste, had not been in the race? Many white voters, feeling that Stokes could not win in a two-man race, might not have bothered to vote at all, so perhaps Stokes would have won by an even larger margin. Thus Stokes's inroad into the white vote was not the decisive factor in his primary victory, although it was important.

Stokes emerged from the primary as the odds-on favorite to win—five weeks later—in the general election. And in the first few days of the campaign, it seemed that Stokes had everything going for him.

■ Stokes was bright, handsome, and articulate. His opponent, Seth Taft, while bright, had never won an election, and his family name, associated with the Taft-Hartley Act, could hardly be an advantage among union members. In addition, he was shy and seemingly uncomfortable in a crowd.

■ Both the *Plain Dealer* and the *Cleveland Press* endorsed Stokes in the general election.

■ The wounds of the primary were quickly (if perhaps superficially) healed, and the Democratic candidates was endorsed by both the Democratic Party and Mayor Locher.

■ Labor—both the A.F.L.-C.I.O. and the Teamsters— also endorsed Stokes.

■ He had a partisan advantage. Of the 326,003 registered voters, only 34,000 (10 percent) were Republican. The closest any Republican mayoral candidate had come to winning was in 1951, when—in a small turnout—William J. McDermott received 45 percent of the vote.

■ Stokes had 90,000 or more Negro votes virtually assured, with little possibility that Taft would make more than slight inroads.

■ Perhaps most important, voting-behavior studies over the years have demonstrated that voters who are confronted by a dilemma react by staying home from the polls. Large numbers of life-long Democrats, faced with voting for a Negro or a Republican by the name of Taft, were likely to stay home.

Had this been a normal election, Democrat Carl Stokes would have won handily. But this was not destined to be a normal election. During the final days of the campaign, Stokes knew he was in a fight for his political life. Those who predicted that the cross-pressures would keep many voters away from the polls forgot that the variable "Negro" had never been involved in an election of this importance.

On Election Day, an estimated 90 percent of those who voted for Locher or Celeste in the Democratic primary shifted to Taft—many pulling a Republican lever for the first time in their life. Was this clearly and unequivocally bigoted backlash? To be sure, bigotry *did* play a major role in the election. But to dismiss the campaign and the election as pure overt bigotry is to miss the significance of what happened in Cleveland and the emerging subtle nature of prejudice in American society.

A closer look at the personal characteristics and campaign strategy of Seth Taft, the Republican candidate, reveals the complexity and subtlety of the race issue.

In the final days of the Democratic primary campaign, Taft repeatedly told reporters that he would rather run against Locher and his record than against Carl Stokes. On the evening of the primary, Taft appeared at Stokes's headquarters to congratulate him. As far as he was concerned, Taft said, the campaign issue was, Who could present the most constructive program for change in Cleveland? Further, he said he didn't want people voting for him simply because he was white. A few days later, Taft even presented a strongly-worded statement to his campaign workers:

"The Cuyahoga Democratic party has issued a number of vicious statements concerning the candidacy of Carl Stokes, and others have conducted whisper campaigns. We cannot tolerate injection of race into this campaign. . . . Many people will vote for Carl Stokes because he is a Negro. Many people will vote for me because I am white. I regret this fact. I will work hard to convince people they should not vote on a racial basis."

Seth Taft's programs to solve racial tensions may have been paternalistic, not really perceptive of emerging moods of the ghetto. But one thing is clear—he was not a bigot. Every indication is that he remained uncomfortable about being in a race in which his chances to win depended, in large part, upon a backlash vote.

Whether Taft's attempt to silence the race issue was

a deliberate strategy or a reflection of deep personal feelings, it probably enhanced his chances of winning. He knew that he had the hard-core bigot vote. His task was to convince those in the middle that they could vote for him and *not* be bigots.

Stokes, on the other hand, had another kind of problem. While he had to draw more white votes, he also had to retain and, if possible, increase the 73 percent Negro turnout that had delivered him 96 percent of the Negro votes in the primary. Stokes's campaign leaders feared a fall-off in the voter turnout from Negro wards—with good reason. The entire primary campaign had pushed the October 3 date so hard that some Negroes could not understand why Carl Stokes was not mayor on October 4. Full-page newspaper ads paid for by CORE had stated, *"If you don't vote Oct. 3rd, forget it. The man who wins will be the next mayor of Cleveland!"* So Stokes felt he had to re-mobilize the Negro vote.

The moment came during the question-and-answer period of the second of four debates with Taft in the all-white westside. Stokes said:

"The personal analysis of Seth Taft—and the analysis of many competent political analysts—is that Seth Taft may win the November 7 election, but for only one reason. That reason is that his skin happens to be white."

The predominantly white crowd booed loudly and angrily for several minutes, and throughout the rest of the evening repeatedly interrupted him. Later, Stokes's campaign manager revealed that his candidate's remark was a calculated risk to arouse Negro interest. Stokes probably succeeded, but he also gave Taft supporters an excuse to bring the race issue into the open.

And they could claim that it was *Stokes,* not Taft, who was trying to exploit the race issue.

To be sure, *both* candidates exploited the race issue. But, for the most part, it was done rather subtly. Stokes's campaign posters stated, "Let's do Cleveland Proud"—another way of saying, "Let's show the world that Cleveland is capable of rising above racial bigotry." A full-page ad for Stokes stated in bold print, "Vote for Seth Taft. It Would Be Easy, Wouldn't It?" After the debate, Taft was free to accuse Stokes of using the race issue—itself a subtle way of exploiting the issue. Then there was the letter, signed by the leaders of 22 nationality clubs, that was mailed to 40,000 members in the city. It didn't mention race, but comments such as "protecting our way of life," "safeguard our liberty," and "false charges of police brutality" were blatant in their implications. Taft sidestepped comment on the letter.

No matter how much the candidates may have wanted to keep race out of the picture, race turned out to be the most important issue. Both Taft and Stokes could benefit from the issue if they played it right, and both did use it. And although the Stokes's remark at the second debate gave white voters an excuse to vote for Taft without feeling that they were bigots, many whites probably would have found another excuse.

The fact is that Taft, for all his lackluster qualities, emerged as a strong candidate. He was able to turn many of his liabilities into assets.

■ Taft was able to insulate himself against his Republican identity. He successfully dissociated himself from his uncle's position on labor by pointing to his own active role, as a student, against "right to work" laws. At the same time, he hit hard at Stokes's record

as an off again-on again Democrat. This strategy neu-
tralized, at least in part, Taft's first political disadvantage—running as a Republican in a Democratic
city.

■ A second liability was that he came from a wealthy
family. Taft was an Ivy League intellectual, cast in
the role of a "do-gooder." He lived in an exclusive
suburb, Pepper Pike, and had bought a modest home
in Cleveland only a few weeks before declaring his
candidacy. How, it was frequently asked, could such a
man understand the problems of the inner-city and of
the poor? Almost invariably the answer was: "Did
John F. Kennedy, Franklin D. Roosevelt, and Nelson
Rockefeller have to be poor in order to understand
and respond to the problems of the poor?" Taft's
campaign posters were a side profile that bore a
striking resemblance to President Kennedy. Whether
he was consciously exploiting the Kennedy image is
an open question. But there can be little doubt that
when Taft mentioned his Republican heritage, he
tried to project an image of the new breed of Republican—John Lindsay and Charles Percy. This image
didn't come across very well at first, but as he became
a seasoned campaigner it became clearer.

■ Another liability was that Taft had never held an
elected office. His opponent tried to exploit this—
unsuccessfully. Taft could point to 20 years of active
civic service, including the fact that he was one of
the authors of the Ohio fair-housing law. Then too,
the charge gave Taft an opportunity to point out that
Stokes had the worst absentee record of anyone in
the state legislature. Stokes never successfully answered
this charge until the last of their four debates, when he
produced a pre-campaign letter from Taft commend-

TABLE II—Percent Stokes Vote by Ward

WHITE WARDS	% Negro	1965 General	1967 Primary	1967 General
1	.6	3.2	17.2	20.5
2	.3	1.9	12.8	17.4
3	.9	2.5	13.6	22.1
4	.3	3.0	18.2	20.9
5	.6	1.7	11.8	17.8
6	.8	2.3	15.1	16.7
7	.6	3.4	16.5	23.7
8	3.0	6.1	24.7	29.3
9	.2	1.9	12.4	16.4
14	1.4	1.1	12.7	13.0
15	1.4	1.2	9.2	14.1
22	5.7	8.1	22.5	26.3
26	1.1	2.8	16.3	19.9
32	2.4	2.9	10.0	15.3
33	.3	2.5	17.7	21.4
Average		3.0	15.2	19.3

NEGRO WARDS				
10	91.3	88.7	97.3	96.7
11	91.8	86.3	95.9	96.0
12	82.7	76.9	90.4	90.5
13	75.2	75.8	90.7	88.4
17	99.0	86.6	98.1	97.9
18	89.3	84.0	96.0	95.7
20	91.0	83.0	95.0	92.8
24	92.6	90.6	98.1	98.1
25	90.9	91.3	98.4	98.2
27	85.7	85.2	95.6	94.0
Average		85.4	96.2	95.0

MIXED WARDS				
16	56.6	50.7	69.9	70.1
19	25.3	29.2	48.0	39.9
21	61.1	55.2	66.3	68.9
23	20.3	9.8	18.2	23.2
28	28.5	26.5	54.8	57.3
29	24.4	26.8	43.2	42.3
30	51.7	51.5	75.3	71.4
31	21.8	16.9	31.8	39.0
Average		35.0	54.4	54.1

ing him on his legislative service. But this came mo-
ments *after* the TV cameras had gone off the air.

■ Still another liability emerged during the campaign. Taft's strategy of discussing programs, not
personalities, was seemingly getting him nowhere. He
presented specific proposals; Stokes, a skilled debater,
succeeded in picking them apart. Stokes himself discussed programs only at a general level and contended that he was best-qualified to "cut the red tape"
in Washington. His frequent trips to Washington to
confer with top Government officials, before and during the campaign, indicated that he had the inside
track.

Taft, realizing at this point that his campaign was
not gaining much momentum, suddenly switched gears
and began attacking Stokes's record (not Stokes per-
sonally). Stokes had claimed he would crack-down on
slumlords. Taft discovered that Stokes owned a piece
of rental property with several code violations—and
that it had not been repaired despite an order from the
city. He hit hard at Stokes's absenteeism and his record
as a "good" Democrat. He put a "bird-dog" on Stokes
and, if Stokes told one group one thing and another
group something else, the public heard about it.

The upshot was that in the final days of the campaign Taft captured the momentum. Stokes was easily
the more flashy debater and projected a superior image;
but Taft emerged as the better strategist.

One may ask whether all of this discussion is really
relevant, since the final vote was sharply divided along
racial lines. In one sense it *is* irrelevant, since it is
possible that a weaker candidate than Taft might have
run just as well. It is also possible that a white racist
might actually have won. Still, this discussion has but-

tressed two important points.

■ Taft was not all black, and Stokes was not all white. Taft proved a strong candidate, and—had he been running against Locher instead of Stokes—he might have amassed strong support from Negroes and defeated Locher.

■ By being a strong candidate, Taft made it much easier for many white Democrats, who might otherwise been cross-pressured into staying home, to come out and vote for him.

Some people felt that Taft should have withdrawn and let Stokes run uncontested. But many of the same people also decried white liberals who, at recent conferences to form coalitions between black-power advocates and the New Left, let black militants castrate them. It is not traditional in American politics that candidates enter a race to lose. Taft was in to win, and he fought a hard and relatively clean campaign—as high a compliment as can be paid to any candidate.

Yet all of this doesn't change the basic nature of the voting. This is clear from the evidence in Table II. Stokes won by holding his black bloc, and increasing his white vote from 15 percent in the primary to almost 20 percent in the general. An enormous amount of the white vote was, whether covert or overt, anti-Negro. It is hard to believe that Catholics, ethnic groups, and laborers who never voted for anyone but a Democrat should suddenly decide to evaluate candidates on their qualifications and programs, and—in overwhelming numbers—decide that the Republican candidate was better qualified. The implication is that they were prejudiced. But to assume that such people perceive themselves as bigots is to oversimplify the nature of prejudice. And to call such people bigots is to make their responses even more rigid—as Carl Stokes discovered after his remark in the second debate with Taft.

This, then, is perhaps an important lesson of the Cleveland election: Bigotry cannot be defeated directly, by telling bigots that they are bigoted. For the most part Stokes learned this lesson well, accumulating as many as 30,000 white votes, nearly five times the number he received in 1965. But another slip like the one in the second debate might have cost him the election.

A few words on the voting for Stokes ward by ward, as shown in the table. Wards 9, 14, and 15— which gave Stokes a comparatively low vote—have the highest concentration of ethnic groups in the city. Not only is there the historical element of prejudice in these areas, but there is the ever-present fear among the residents that Negroes will invade their neighborhoods. (This fear is less a factor in ward 9, which is across the river.)

Wards 26 and 32 also gave Stokes a low percentage of votes, and these wards are also the ones most likely to have Negro migration. They are just to the north of East Cleveland, which is currently undergoing heavy transition, and to the east of ward 27, which in the past few years has changed from white to black. In these two wards, then, high ethnic composition and a fear of Negro migration would seem to account for Stokes's 19.9 and 15.3 percentages.

The highest percentage *for* Stokes in predominantly white areas was in wards 8 and 22. Ward 8 has a growing concentration of Puerto Ricans, and—according to newspaper polls—they voted heavily for Stokes. Ward 22 has a very large automobile-assembly plant that employs many Negroes. Now, in 1965 the ward was 5.7 percent Negro—a large increase from 1960. Since 1965, this percentage has probably grown another 2 or 3 percent. Therefore, if one subtracts the Negro vote that Stokes received in this ward, the size of the white vote is about the same as in other wards.

The race for mayor in Gary, Ind., was not overtly racist. Still, the racial issue was much less subtle than it was in Cleveland. When Democratic chairman John G. Krupa refused to support Richard D. Hatcher, the Democratic candidate, it was clear that the reason was race. When the Gary newspaper failed to give similar coverage to both candidates and sometimes failed to print news releases from Hatcher headquarters (ostensibly because press deadlines had not been met), it was clear that race was a factor.

Even though race was rarely mentioned openly, the city polarized. While Stokes had the support of the white-owned newspapers and many white campaign workers, many of Hatcher's white supporters preferred to remain in the background—in part, at least, because they feared reprisals from white racists. Hatcher didn't use the black-power slogan, but to the community the election was a contest between black and white. And when the Justice Department supported Hatcher's claim that the election board had illegally removed some 5000 Negro voters from the registration lists and added nonexistent whites, the tension in the city became so great that the Governor, feeling that there was "imminent danger" of violence on election night, called up 4000 National Guardsmen.

Negroes constitute an estimated 55 percent of Gary's 180,000 residents, but white voter registration outnumbers Negroes by 2000 or 3000. Like Stokes, Hatcher—in order to win—had to pull some white votes, or have a significantly higher Negro turnout.

The voter turnout and voting patterns in Cleveland and Gary were very similar. In both cities, almost 80 percent of the registered voters turned out at the polls. In the Glen Park and Miller areas, predominantly white neighborhoods, Joseph B. Radigan—Hatcher's opponent—received more than 90 percent of the votes. In the predominantly Negro areas, Hatcher received an estimated 93 percent of the votes. In all, Hatcher received about 4000 white votes, while losing probably 1000 Negro votes, at most, to Radigan. This relatively small white vote was enough to give him victory. If Stokes's miscalculation in bringing race into the Cleveland campaign gave prejudiced whites an excuse to vote for Taft, the glaring way the Democratic Party in Gary tried to defeat Hatcher probably tipped the scales and gave Hatcher some white votes he wouldn't have received otherwise.

The Boston election, unlike the Cleveland and Gary elections, didn't pose a Negro against a white, but a lackluster candidate—Kevin White—against a 48-year-old grandmother who had gained national attention over the past several years for her stand against school integration. On the surface, Mrs. Hicks seems to be an obvious racial bigot. But she herself has repeatedly denied charges that she is a racist, and many who have followed her closely claim that this description is too simple.

Mrs. Hicks, perhaps more than any other public figure to emerge in recent years, reflects the complex and subtle nature of prejudice in America. Her public denial of bigotry is, in all probability, an honest expression of her self-image. But she is basically unaware of, and unwilling to become informed about, the way her views maintain the barriers of segregation and discrimination in American society. In 1963, when the N.A.A.C.P. asked the Boston School Committee to acknowledge the *de facto* segregation in the schools, she refused to review the evidence. Meeting with the N.A.A.C.P., she abruptly ended the discussion by proclaiming: "There is no *de facto* segregation in Boston's schools. Kindly proceed to educational matters." Later, when the State Board of Education presented a 132-page report on racial imbalance in Massachusetts schools, she lashed out at the report's recommendations without bothering to read it.

Mrs. Hicks, like millions of Americans, holds views on race that are born out of and perpetuated by ignorance. John Spiegel, director of Brandeis University's Lemberg Center for the Study of Violence, has summed up the preliminary report of its study of six cities:

". . . the attitude of whites seems to be based on ignorance of or indifference to the factual basis of Negro resentment and bitterness. . . . If white populations generally had a fuller appreciation of the just grievances and overwhelming problems of Negroes in the ghetto, they would give stronger support to their city governments to promote change and to correct the circumstances which give rise to strong feelings of resentment now characteristic of ghetto populations."

Prejudice is born not only out of ignorance, but also out of fear. There is much about the Negro ghettos of poverty that causes whites, lacking objective knowledge, to be afraid, and their fear in turn reinforces their prejudice and their inability to hear out and understand the plight of the Negro in America.

In Boston, the voter turnout was heavy (71 percent) but below the turnouts in Cleveland and Gary. White accumulated 53 percent of the vote and a 12,000 plurality. Compared with Stokes and Hatcher, he had an easy victory. But considering Mrs. Hicks's lack of qualifications and the racial overtones of her campaign, Boston also experienced a massive backlash vote. Had it not been for the final days of the campaign—when she pledged, unrealistically, to raise police and firemen's salaries to $10,000 without raising taxes, and came back from Washington with "positive assurance" that nonexistent Federal monies would cover the raises —she might even have won. But throughout the campaign Mrs. Hicks repeatedly revealed her ignorance of fiscal and political matters. Mrs. Hicks had another handicap: She is a woman. The incredible fact that she ran a close race demonstrated again the hard core of prejudice and ignorance in American society.

Now let us consider the broader implications these elections will have on the racial crisis in America. To be sure, the immediate implications are quite different from what they would have been if Stokes and Hatcher had lost and Mrs. Hicks had won. If the elections had gone the other way, Summer '68 might well have begun November 8. As Thomas Pettigrew of Harvard put it a few days before the election, "If Stokes and Hatcher lose and Mrs. Hicks wins, then I just wonder how a white man in this country could ever look a Negro in the eye and say, 'Why don't you make it the way we did, through the political system, rather than burning us down?' "

But do these victories really alter the basic nature of the racial crisis? There is, true, some reason for hope. But to assume that anything has been fundamentally altered would be disastrous. First of all, it is by no means clear that these elections will pacify militant Negroes—including those in Cleveland, Gary, and Boston. In Boston, some militants were even encouraging people to vote for Mrs. Hicks—because they felt that her victory would help unify the Negro community against a well-defined foe. In Cleveland, most militants remained less than enthusiastic about the possibility of a Stokes victory. Of the militant groups, only CORE worked hard for him. In Gary alone did the candidate have the solid support of militants—probably because Hatcher refused to explicitly rebuke Stokely Carmichael and H. Rap Brown, and because his opponents repeatedly claimed that Hatcher was a black-power advocate.

If the Stokes and Hatcher victories are to represent a turning point in the racial crisis, they must deliver results. Unfortunately, Hatcher faces an unsympathetic Democratic Party and city council. Stokes has gone a long way toward healing the wounds of the bitter primary, but it remains to be seen whether he will receive eager support for his programs. Some councilmen from ethnic wards will almost certainly buck his programs for fear of alienating their constituencies.

Stokes and Hatcher themselves face a difficult and delicate situation.

■ Their margins of victory were so narrow that they, like Kennedy in 1960, must proceed with great caution.

■ Enthusiasm and promises of change are not the same as the power to implement change. And the two mayors must share power with whites.

■ They must demonstrate to Negroes that their presence in City Hall has made a difference. But if their programs seem too preferential toward Negroes, they run the risk of massive white resistance.

This delicate situation was clearly seen in the early days of the Stokes administration. Of his first ten appointments, only two were Negroes. Although relations with the police have been one of the most sensitive issues in the Negro ghetto, Stokes's choice for a new police chief was Michael Blackwell, a 67-year-old "hardliner." This appointment was intended to ease anxieties in the ethnic neighborhoods, but it was not popular in the Negro ghetto. Blackwell, in his first public address after being sworn in, lashed out at the Supreme Court, state laws, and "publicity-seeking clergy and beatniks" for "crippling law enforcement." Cleveland's Negroes are already beginning to wonder whether a Negro in City Hall is going to make any difference.

Some observers believe that Stokes is basically quite conservative, and point to his sponsorship of anti-riot legislation. To be sure, Stokes's position on many issues remains uncertain, but what does seem fairly clear from his early days in office is that his efforts to gain support in white communities is going to lead to disaffection among Negroes. How much and how quickly is a difficult question.

Race relations is only one of many problems that these two new mayors must face. Stokes has inherited all of the problems that brought national attention to Cleveland last spring—poverty, urban renewal, finance, transportation, air and water pollution, and so on. Hatcher faces similar problems in Gary, and must also cope with one of the nation's worst strongholds of organized crime. If they fail, the responsibility will fall heavier on them than had a white man failed.

Some whites will generalize the failures to all Negro politicians, and some Negroes will generalize the failures to the "bankruptcy" of the American political system.

Almost certainly, Washington will be a key factor in determining if these two men succeed. The national Democratic Party has a strong interest in making Stokes and Hatcher look good, for it desperately needs to recapture the disaffected Negro voters before the 1968 national election. But how much can the party deliver? The war in Vietnam is draining enormous national resources and Congress is threatening to slash poverty programs. Even if Federal monies were no problem, there is the question whether *any* of Washington's existing programs are directed at the roots of ghetto unrest. Many informed administrators, scientists, and political analysts feel they are not. And the chances for creative Federal programs seem, at this moment, fairly dim.

Another clear implication of these elections is that white resistance to change remains large and widespread. More than 90 percent of the Democrats in Cleveland who voted for a Democrat in the primary switched, in the general election, to the Republican candidate. Now, not many American cities are currently composed of as many as 35 percent Negroes; the possibility of coalitions to elect other Negro candidates appears, except in a handful of cities, remote. Additional Negro mayoral candidates are almost certain to arise, and many will go down to bitter defeat.

Stokes and Hatcher won because black-voter power coalesced with a relatively small minority of liberal whites. It was not a victory of acceptance or even tolerance of Negroes, but a numerical failure of the powers of discrimination, a failure that resulted in large part because of the massive exodus of whites from the central city. The election of Stokes and Hatcher may break down white resistance to voting for a Negro, but this is, at best, problematical. Also problematical is how bigoted whites will react to the election of a Negro mayor. Their organized efforts to resist change may intensify. As we have already indicated, the pace of white exodus from the central city of Cleveland is already alarming. And an acceleration of this pace could push the city into financial bankruptcy.

In short, while the implications of the November 7 elections are ambiguous, it does seem that the victories of Stokes and Hatcher, and the defeat of Mrs. Hicks, have kept the door open on the growing racial crisis. America has, at best, bought a little time.

On the other hand, we do not find much cause for optimism in those elections—unlike George Meany, and unlike the *New York Times,* which, five days after the election, published a glowing editorial about "the willingness of most voters today to choose men solely on personal quality and impersonal issues." To us, it would seem that the elections have only accelerated the pace of ever-rising expectations among Negroes. And if results don't follow, and rather rapidly, then we believe that the Negro community's frustration with the American political system will almost certainly heighten.

The hard task of demonstrating that Negroes can actually achieve justice and equality in America still lies ahead.

January/February 1968

Black Power
At the Ballot Box

Review-essay of
Negroes and the New Southern Politics
by Donald R. Matthews and James W. Prothro
(New York: Harcourt, Brace & World, 1966)
AUGUST MEIER

In this ambitious work, the authors have taken a critical look at the thesis advanced by journalists, civil rights leaders, and politicians that the franchise would be "the southern Negro's strongest and most accessible weapon in his struggle for full citizenship," that "the vote will automatically give southern Negroes influence over public policy commensurate with their numbers," thus affording them the "political leverage" to eliminate discrimination.

Defining political participation as "all behavior through which people directly express their political opinions"— from talking about politics to seeking office—the authors set out to do four things:

(1) to describe the political activities of southern Negroes;

(2) to explain why some of them participate in politics while many do not;

(3) to try to predict the future of Negro political participation in the South;

(4) to explore the likely fruits of this political activity.

In approaching their task the authors combine an elaborate statistical analysis with intensive studies of four illustrative (though admittedly not representative) areas—a county in Mississippi, another largely rural county in the Virginia-North Carolina tobacco belt, and two unidentified cities: "Urbania" (Durham) and "Capital City" (Tallahassee), both of which lie in the "peripheral" rather than in the "Deep" South.

The discussion of the four illustrative communities—much of it evidently based on the earlier research of Lewis Killian for Tallahassee and Elaine Burgess for Durham—proves more illuminating in regard to the actual dynamics involved in Negro political activity in different kinds of southern communities than do the mountains of statistics, the impressive mathematical manipulations, and the scores of elegant graphs derived from four or five years of research and analysis.

The generalizations which Matthews and Prothro draw from their data will be, in the main, familiar to knowledgeable observers.

Some examples: that "both formal voter requirements and the manner in which they are administered are strongly related to variations in Negro voter registration"; that the usual correlation between education and political participation is to some extent reversed among southern Negroes, because the majority of Negro college graduates are teachers —the most vulnerable and therefore the most conservative group in the Negro community; that the Deep South and the Peripheral South possess two distinct political subcultures; that Negro registration is low, "in rather large part, because of the social and economic characteristics of Southern communities."

On Negro Leadership: "Our analysis has identified three

general types of Negro leaders in the South: *traditional* leaders, who seek ameliorative action from whites within the system of segregation; *moderates,* whose goal is to improve the welfare of Negroes through gradual desegregation; and *militants,* who are dedicated to psychic victories and the immediate destruction of racial segregation ... [;] Negro leaders who pursue these differing goals tend also to differ in their strategies and tactics, sources of influence, and recruitment patterns"; and, except in the most backward of Southern communities, Negro leaders possess either high status or economic independence from whites, with half of those interviewed possessing both.

On the Future: There is an alarming divergence of Negro and white attitudes and expectations that may end in violence; there is a tragic out-migration of potential college-educated Negro leaders; in pursuing their economic goals, Negroes will be likely to find their political allies among the virulent working-class segregationists, while in pursuing their status goals (desegregation and equal constitutional rights), they are most likely to find allies among the middle-class, economically conservative whites.

There is nothing dubious about any of these rather obvious generalizations. The question, however, does arise: were the four or five years of research and analysis of statistical data really necessary to establish them?

The conclusions about the effectiveness of Negro participation in southern politics in the foreseeable future are essentially pessimistic. Negroes are bound to find their high expectations frustrated unless southern whites move far more rapidly than they are doing toward acceptance of desegregation and protection of the Negroes' constitutional rights. Even in areas where they do vote freely, Negroes are weak in all political resources except the number of votes they can muster. Yet even in this respect they are at a disadvantage, because in every southern state, and in the vast majority of southern counties, Negroes are in a minority. As a minority they will have to form coalitions with white political factions; but as the authors point out in one of their most illuminating and original sections, only under certain conditions will such coalitions be feasible. Consequently, even if—as is most likely—the number of registered Negroes continues to increase, only relatively rarely will they be able to achieve sufficient political leverage to significantly improve their situation.

Some hope does stem from two major factors. One is that "the politics of race and the politics of class now divide the southern electorate in somewhat different ways; the noncongruence of these political cleavages tends to dampen and moderate the effects of both." (Both most Negroes and the highly segregationist working-class whites have common economic interests which incline them to support the national Democratic party.) Second, the authors predict increasing federal intervention, which they regard as a far more powerful force for social change than the votes of Negroes in southern state and local elections.

Within the South itself, the authors hold that Negroes can bring about improvements only through highly resilient and skillful leaders who are capable of making pragmatic and flexible coalitions with various white factions as the opportunity arises. The prototype for this type of activity has been the relatively successful history of the Durham Committee on Negro Affairs. Yet even this technique has limitations, for "opponents of biracial coalitions need merely take steps to increase the salience of the racial issue to the electorate at large, and the Negro-white coalition usually dissolves."

The authors' interpretation thus places a high priority on moderate leadership, such as has characterized the dominant figures among Durham Negroes. Matthews and Prothro are highly critical both of the old-fashioned "Uncle Tom," whose influence depends upon his ability to wheedle small favors out of white officials, and of the militants, like the Rev. C. K. Steele of Tallahassee, whose actions they feel have served to polarize the situation and make progress through compromise impossible. In short, astute Negro bloc voting is essential, but "black power" ideology must be avoided. And even astute moderate leadership will not bring the millennium in a hurry. At best, the concrete payoffs from Negro voting will be modest indeed.

With their affinity for consensus and moderation, Matthews and Prothro seriously underestimate both the role of the militants and the functions of disunity within the Negro leadership. For example, in the case of Durham, they do mention in passing references that the militants were influential in pushing the established Negro leadership into a more radical stance, but the authors do not appear to attach much importance to the fact that there and elsewhere the militants have usually served the exceedingly important function of upsetting the whites and thereby legitimizing the position and demands of the moderates.

In their effort to give a sober and realistic appraisal of what Negroes can expect to gain from participation in southern politics, I feel that the authors may have actually underestimated the impact that voting at the local level can have in furthering the goals of the Negro community. It has been my observation, for example, that wherever the college student demonstrations were successful in 1960-1961, Negroes were a significant part of the electorate. With the data at their disposal, Matthews and Prothro could probably have easily tested the validity of this proposition.

I also find factual errors that reveal inadequate knowledge of southern history, of the subculture of the Negro community, and of the civil rights movement. The authors reveal their lack of sophistication by referring to the journalistic and distorted "quickie," Louis Lomax's *The Negro Revolt,* and the polemical and hyperbolic essay, E. Franklin Frazier's *Black Bourgeoisie,* as if they were scholarly works. They have "relied heavily" on an outdated work, Paul Lewinson's *Race, Class and Party,* published in 1932, and come up with the hoary and discredited myth that during Reconstruction "for a time, the southern electorate was predominantly black; the South was ruled by a coalition of former slaves and their northern sympathizers. Even friendly observers agreed that the government of the region was extravagant, corrupt, and incompetent." They attribute Negro constitutional disfranchisement in the late 19th century to southern "Bourbons" who feared Populism, but ignore the role which Populists themselves often played in pressing for these laws, and the support that Negroes often found among southern conservatives. Again, in accounting for the decline in Negro registration in the mid-1950's (following the upswing after the white primary was outlawed in 1944), Matthews and Prothro stress white resistance to the 1954 Supreme Court school decision, but fail to mention that in parts of the Deep South whites were becoming alarmed by the growth of the Negro electorate itself.

More serious are the authors' misconceptions about the history and nature of Negro protest. One cannot seriously fault them for not dealing with the largely esoteric history of Negro direct-action prior to World War II, though their failure to mention the 1941 March on Washington is unfortunate. But to ignore the whole early history of CORE, founded in 1942 (which they consistently refer to incorrectly as the Congress *on* Racial Equality, and in one place as the *Committee* on Racial Equality); to characterize the organization's early work as concentrating on housing segregation in the North; to say that the first organized sit-in was held in Wichita, Kansas, in 1958; and to practically dismiss CORE's Miami, Florida, sit-ins of 1959 (while failing to mention CORE activity prior to 1960 in other parts of the Peripheral South) together constitute a major series of errors and omissions. And then to top it off by stating that the four freshmen at North Carolina A. & T. College in 1960 "managed to create a region-wide 'movement' from what had been scattered and sporadic protests" not only gives an erroneous notion about the way the student movement of 1960 developed, but displays an extraordinary naiveté about the nature of social causation as well.

Finally, I have serious reservations about Matthews and Prothro's characterization of the Negro college student protesters of 1960-1961. In certain major particulars their statistical data are sharply at variance with my own extensive observations of college student action groups from Baltimore to New Orleans. The authors found that upperclassmen and males were disproportionately represented in the student movement; I found that freshmen and women were disproportionately active. The authors indicate that the better educated students were more likely to be active, while my experiences indicate that the weaker students were those most likely to be participants in the movement. Matthews and Prothro maintain that the low-income students participated about as much as, or less—but not more —than the higher income students; my observations indicate that the low-income students were the ones more likely to participate. In fact, many of the student protest leaders themselves characterized the type of student who was involved in the movement as belonging to the "striving lower class." Perhaps upward mobility aspirations were more important than social class background in leading students to participate in the movement. There were variations, of course, and at some of the colleges the more elite students made up a substantial portion of the body of protesters. Nor would I presume to question the authors' sample (although it would have been helpful if they had followed the procedure they used in their study of adult political participation, and supplemented their statistical data with intensive examination of a few colleges as illustrative case-studies). I suspect that the major reason for the discrepancy lies in the fact that Matthews and Prothro failed to distinguish between students who joined in demonstrations once or twice, and those who engaged in them over a sustained period. I believe that if they had measured this variable, they would have found the profile of the really dedicated protesters to be quite different from that of those whose involvement was of a more casual variety. And it is the former group, after all, which was really the backbone of the student movement and the principal dynamic thrust within it. At any rate, the question deserves careful further study.

The authors have supported most effectively their fundamental proposition that the vote will bring only modest and gradual gains for southern Negroes. Generally speaking, the book is a welcome contribution to the literature, a provocative work that will excite discussion among scholars for some time to come. My principal criticism is that the authors are so enamored of moderation, so wedded to consensus politics, that they have sharply underestimated the contribution and role of the militants. This underlying bias may well account for the authors' ignorance about CORE. The book almost seems to be a deliberate attempt to refute the persuasive arguments of Killian and Grigg's remarkable volume, *Racial Crisis in America,* which brilliantly demonstrates the function of realistic social conflict in improving the Negroes' status, though it unfortunately denies the importance of factors encouraging consensus. Apparently there is still a need for the behavioral scientist who will combine into a single model the conflict and consensus theories of social change in American race relations.

October 1967

What Black Power Means to Negroes in Mississippi

JOYCE LADNER

For three months during the summer of last year, I conducted a study aimed at finding out how Mississippi Negroes who endorsed "black power" interpreted this new concept. I learned that even those civil-rights activists who welcomed the concept attached curiously different meanings to it. My research also helped me understand why the black-power slogan proved so welcome to these activists— and why its acceptance was accompanied by the expulsion of whites from positions of leadership. Finally, my investigation provided some hints on the usefulness of the black-power slogan in helping Mississippi Negroes achieve their goals.

The black-power concept that emerged during the past year created fierce controversy, not only among white liberals but among Negro activists and conservatives. Most of the nation's top civil-rights leaders denounced the slogan —or vigorously embraced it. Instead of "black power,"

Martin Luther King Jr. advocated the acquisition of "power for all people." The N.A.A.C.P.'s Roy Wilkins, in condemning the slogan, used such terms as "anti-white power . . . a reverse Hitler . . . a reverse Ku Klux Klan and . . . can only mean black death." On the other hand, Stokely Carmichael, former head of SNCC, was the chief advocate of the slogan, which he defined as "the ability of black people to politically get together and organize themselves so that they can speak from a position of strength rather than a position of weakness." CORE's Floyd McKissick agreed.

But though Negro civil-rights leaders were divided about black power, the slogan was welcomed by many disenchanted Negroes living in Northern ghettos. These Negroes tended to view black power as a tangible goal that, when acquired, would lift them from their inferior positions in the social structure. Still, despite the positive identification that Negroes in the Northern ghettos had with the rhetoric of black power, SNCC and CORE made no massive attempts to involve these Negroes in black-power programs.

But what about the South? How did Negroes in Mississippi, and civil-rights organizations in Mississippi, interpret the new slogan? This was what I wanted to find out.

I used two methods of study. The first was *participant-observation*—in informal, small meetings of civil-rights activists; in civil-rights rallies; and in protest demonstrations, including the historic Meredith march. The second was the *focused interview*. I chose to interview 30 Negroes who, I had found, were in favor of black power. All were friends or acquaintances of mine, and all had had long experience in Southern civil-rights work. They represented about two-thirds of the black-power leaders in the state. (My personal involvement with the civil-rights movement helped provide the rapport needed to acquire the observational data, as well as the interview data.)

Among other things, I learned that many Negro activists in Mississippi had immediately embraced the black-power slogan—because of the already widely-held belief that power *was* an effective tool for obtaining demands from the ruling elite in Mississippi. Since 1960, civil-rights organizations have been playing a major role in involving Mississippi Negroes in the fight for equality. As a result, these Negroes became more and more dissatisfied with their impoverished, powerless positions in the social structure. The 1960 census reports that the median family income for Mississippi Negroes (who constitute 42.3 percent of Mississippi's population) was $1168, as opposed to $3565 for whites. Until fewer than five years ago, only 6 percent of the eligible Negroes were registered to vote. Today, the traditional all-white primary still exists—in almost the same form as it did 25 years ago. Since many of the efforts Mississippi Negroes made to change the social structure—through integration—were futile, they began to reconceptualize their fight for equality from a different perspective, one designed to acquire long-sought goals through building bases of power.

The black-power concept was, then, successfully communicated to Mississippi Negroes because of the failure of integration. But it was also communicated to them by the shooting of James Meredith on his march through Mississippi. This act of violence made Negro activists feel justified in calling for "audacious black power." For only with black power, they contended, would black people be able to prevent events like the shooting.

But there were varying degrees of acceptance of the slogan among Mississippi Negroes. Some, of course, did not accept the slogan at all—those who were never part of the civil-rights movement. Despite the fact that Mississippi has been one of the centers of civil-rights activity in the United States for the past six or seven years, no more than half the Negro population (I would surmise) has ever been actively involved in the movement. In such areas as Sunflower County, a very high percentage of Negroes have participated; but in many other areas, like Laurel, only a small percentage of the Negroes have taken part.

As for those Negroes active in the movement, they can be broadly classified into two groups. The first: the traditional, moderate, N.A.A.C.P.-style activists, who boast of having been "freedom fighters" before the "new movement" came into existence. They include ministers; small-businessmen; professionals; a sizable following of middle-class people; and a small number of the rank and file. Frequently the white ruling elite calls these activists the "responsible" leaders. The primary activities of this group include selling N.A.A.C.P. memberships; initiating legal action against segregation and discriminatory practices; negotiating with the ruling elite; and conducting limited boycotts and voter-registration campaigns.

The second group of activists are the less economically advantaged. Although a small number were once members of the N.A.A.C.P., most of them joined the movement only since 1960. They are readily identified with such organizations as the Freedom Democratic Party, CORE, SNCC, the Delta Ministry, and the Southern Christian Leadership Conference. Members of this group include plantation workers, students, the average lower-class Negro, and a small number of ministers, professionals, and businessmen. More militant than the first group, these activists conduct mass marches, large-scale boycotts, sit-ins, dramatic voter-registration campaigns, and so forth.

Members of the traditional organizations, in sum, are

still committed to working for integration. It is the militants who are oriented toward a black-power ideology, who consider integration irrelevant to what they see as the major task at hand—uniting black people to build black institutions. I suspect that a larger number of activists identify with traditional organizations like the N.A.A.C.P. than with the more militant ones.

The 30 black-power advocates I interviewed were, of course, the militant activists. Even so, I found that even these 30 could be further classified—into categories that Robert K. Merton has called *local* and *cosmopolitan*:

> The localite largely confines his interest to this [town of Rovere] community. Devoting little thought or energy to the Great Society he is preoccupied with local problems, to the virtual exclusion of the national and international scene. He is, strictly speaking, parochial.
>
> Contrariwise with the cosmopolitan type. He has some interest in Rovere and must of course maintain a minimum of relations within the community since he, too, exerts influence there. But he is also oriented significantly to the world outside Rovere and regards himself as an integral part of that world. . . . The cosmopolitan is ecumenical.

In this paper, I shall use "local" to refer to those long-term residents of Mississippi—usually uneducated, unskilled adults—whose strong commitment to civil-rights activity stemmed primarily from their desire to produce massive changes in the "home-front," the area they call home.

I shall use "cosmopolitan" to refer to the urbane, educated, highly skilled young civil-rights activists who are usually newcomers to Mississippi. Because they went to the state to work in the civil-rights movement only temporarily, their identification with the area tends to be weak.

One-third of my respondents, I found, hold the cosmopolitan view. The majority are Negro men, but there are a small group of Negro women and a very small group of white sympathizers. The mean age is about 23 or 24. About half are from the North; the remainder are from Mississippi and other Southern states. Most of the cosmopolitans are formally educated and many have come from middle-class Northern families and gone to the better universities. They are widely read and widely traveled. They are also artistic: Writers, painters, photographers, musicians, and the like are often found in the cosmopolitan group. Their general orientation toward life is an intellectual one. They are associated with SNCC, the Freedom Democratic Party, and CORE. Although a few are actively engaged in organizing black people in the various counties, much of their work in the state is centered on philosophical discussions, writing, and so forth. All of the cosmopolitans have had wide associations with white people. Some grew up and attended school with whites; other had contact with whites in the civil-rights movement. The cosmopolitans maintain that black people in American society must redefine the term "black" and all that it symbolizes, and that black pride and dignity must be implanted in all Negro Americans. The cosmopolitan position embraces the belief that the plight of Negro Americans is comparable to neocolonialized "colored peoples" of the world.

The cosmopolitans' participation in the Southern civil-rights scene, by and large, dates back to 1960 and the beginning of the student movement in the South. Their present ideology has to be viewed in the framework of the history of their involvement in the movement, with special emphasis on the negative experiences they encountered.

Some six years ago, black Americans began to seek their long-desired civil rights with a new sense of urgency. The N.A.A.C.P.'s painstaking effort to obtain legal, theoretical rights for Negroes was challenged. Groups of Negro college students in the South decided to fight the gradualism that had become traditional and to substitute radical action aimed at bringing about rapid social change. These students began their drive for equal rights with lunch-counter demonstrations. After much immediate success, they spread their drive to the political arena. Their only hope for the future, they felt, lay in the ballot. Much to their disappointment, acquiring political power was not so easy as integrating lunch counters. The students met their strongest resistance from whites in full possession of the sought-after political power. To deal with this resistance, the Federal Government passed two civil-rights laws: public accommodation and voting rights. But the Government did little to implement these laws. Still, in the early 1960s, student civil-rights workers had an almost unrelenting faith in the Federal Government and believed that changes in the laws would rapidly pave the way for sweeping changes in the social structure. This was the era when students were much involved in hard-core organizing. They paid little attention to abstract philosophizing. Instead they occupied themselves with such pressing problems as the mass arrests of Negroes in Greenwood, Miss.

As time went on, the cosmopolitans became more and more discouraged about their organizing efforts. They began to seriously question the feasibility of their strategies and tactics. By the end of 1964, after the historic Mississippi Summer Project, the cosmopolitans began to feel that their organizational methods were just not effective. For roughly a year and a half, they groped and searched for more effective strategies. Frequently they felt frustrated; sometimes they despaired. A number of them returned to the North and got well-paying jobs or went to graduate and professional schools. Others were alienated from some of the basic values of American society. Some students developed a strong interest in Africa and began to look to various African states as possible havens. Still others, after deciding that they had accomplished all that was possible through organizations such as SNCC, associated themselves with radical leftist groups.

It was during the tail end of this six-year period that two position papers were written by the cosmopolitans. One was by a group that insisted that Negroes expel whites from leadership roles in civil-rights organizations, and that Negroes develop "black consciousness" and "black nationalism." "Black consciousness" refers to a set of ideas and behavior patterns affirming the beauty of blackness and dispelling any negative images that black people may have incorporated about blackness. "Black nationalism" is a kind of patriotic devotion to the development of the Negro's own political, economic, and social institutions. Black nationalism is *not* a racist ideology with separatist overtones, however, but simply a move toward independence from the dominant group, the whites. This paper states:

> If we are to proceed toward true liberation, we must cut ourselves off from white people. We must form our own institutions, credit unions, co-ops, political parties, write our own histories. . . . SNCC, by allowing whites to remain in the organization, can have its efforts subverted. . . . Indigenous leadership cannot be built with whites in the positions they now hold. They [whites] can participate on a voluntary basis . . . but in no way can they participate on a policy-making level.

In response, one white civil-rights worker—Pat McGauley —wrote a paper acceding to the demands of the black-consciousness group:

> The time has indeed come for blacks and whites in the movement to separate; however, it must always be

kept in mind that the final goal of the revolution we are all working for is a multi-racial society.

The cosmopolitans I interviewed conceived of black power in highly philosophical terms—as an ideology that would unite black people as never before. To most of them, black power was intricately bound up with black consciousness. To a long-time SNCC worker, black consciousness was:

. . . an awareness of oneself as a removed nation of black people who are capable of running and developing their own governments and who have pride in their blackness to the extent that they won't sell out. . . . To the extent that he can say, "I'm no longer ashamed of my blackness." The individual redefines the society's rules in terms of his own being. There is a new kind of awakening of the individual, a new kind of realization of self, a type of security, and a type of self-confidence.

Another cosmopolitan equated black consciousness with community loyalty:

Black consciousness is not the question but rather [the question is] from which community one comes from. If you know that, you can identify with black people anywhere in the world then. That is all that is necessary.

These young people firmly believe that even the term "black" has to be redefined. To one of them, "Black has never had any favorable expression in the English language." To another, "American society has characterized black as the symbol for strength, evil, potency and malignancy. . . . People are afraid of the night, of blackness."

Most cosmopolitans feel that black people must acquire black consciousness before they can successfully develop the tools and techniques for acquiring black power. As one of them put it:

Black consciousness is the developmental stage of

black power. Black power will be incomplete without black consciousness. Black consciousness is basically the search for identity; or working out one's own identity. . . . There must be a long process of learning and un-learning in between and a period of self-questing.

In short, by developing black consciousness, a Negro can appreciate his blackness and thus develop a kind of community loyalty to other colored peoples of the world.

Most of the cosmopolitans felt that the redefinition of blackness must take place in the black community *on the black man's terms.* When such a redefinition has taken place, black men who feel psychologically castrated because of their blackness will be able to compete with whites as psychological equals. ("Psychologically castrated" is a popular term among cosmopolitans, and refers to Negroes whose beliefs and behavior have become so warped by the values of white American society that they have come to regard themselves as inferior.)

Cosmopolitans are familiar with the works of Marcus Garvey, Malcolm X, Franz Fanon, Kwame Nkrumah, and other revolutionary nationalists. Some can quote passages from their works. To the cosmopolitans, Marcus Garvey (1887–1940), who tried to instill racial pride in Negroes, was a pioneer of black nationalism and black consciousness in America. The greatest impact on the cosmopolitans, however, comes from the contemporary Malcolm X, whose philosophy—toward the latter period of his life—reflected a revolutionary spirit and a total dissatisfaction with the plight of Negroes in this country. One of the cosmopolitans had this to say about Malcolm X:

Malcolm was very much together. . . . He was a man who knew what he was doing and would have eventually showed everyone what he was capable of doing. . . . Malcolm had history behind him and was with the cat on the block.

To another:

Malcolm X . . . was able to relate to people and to the press. The press is your right arm. . . . In order to be a real militant, you have to use the man [press] and that is what Malcolm did. They [the press] didn't create Malcolm. . . . The press was attuned to Malcolm. . . . Malcolm was not attuned to the press.

Some cosmopolitans call themselves students of Malcolm X and express the hope that another such leader will soon emerge.

Another symbolic leader is the late Algerian revolutionary, Franz Fanon, whose *The Wretched of the Earth* has become a veritable Bible to the cosmopolitans. Fanon tried to justify the use of violence by the oppressed against the oppressor, and to relate the neocolonialization of the black man in Algeria to the plight of colored peoples everywhere. Similarly, the cosmopolitans have great admiration for Stokely Carmichael, one of their associates, whose philosophy is highlighted in this passage:

The colonies of the United States—and this includes the black ghettos within its borders, north and south—must be liberated. For a century this nation has been like an octopus of exploitation, its tentacles stretching from Mississippi and Harlem to South America, the Middle East, southern Africa, and Vietnam; the form of exploitation varies from area to area but the essential result has been the same—a powerful few have been maintained and enriched at the expense of the poor and voiceless colored masses. This pattern must be broken. As its grip loosens here and there around the world, the hopes of black Americans become more realistic. For racism to die, a totally different America must be born. Embodied within the philosophy of the cosmopolitans is an essential proposition that American society is inherently racist, that the majority of white Americans harbor prejudice against black people. Few make any distinction between whites—for example, the white Southerner as opposed to the Northern liberal. Whites are considered symbolic of the black man's oppression, and therefore one should not differentiate between sympathetic whites and unsympathetic whites. The conclusion of the cosmopolitans is that any sweeping structural changes in American society can come about only through the black man's taking an aggressive role in organizing his political, economic, and social institutions. The black man must control his destiny.

I have categorized the remaining two-thirds of my 30 respondents as locals. (Of what significance these ratios are, by the way, I am not sure.) The locals are almost as committed to solving the pressing problems of inadequate income, education, housing, and second-class citizenship *practically* as the cosmopolitans are committed to solving them *philosophically*. Most of the locals are life-long residents of their communities or other Mississippi communities. Most of them, like the cosmopolitans, have been drawn into the movement only since 1960. Unlike the generally youthful cosmopolitans, the age range of the locals is from young adult to elderly. Many locals are indigenous leaders in their communities and in state-wide organizations. Whereas cosmopolitans tend to be middle-class, locals are members of the lower-class black communities and they range from plantation workers to a few who have acquired modest homes and a somewhat comfortable style of life. Many are leaders in the Mississippi Freedom Democratic Party, which in 1964 challenged the legality of the all-white Mississippi delegation to the national Democratic convention and in 1965 challenged the constitutionality of the elected white Representatives to serve in the U.S. House of Representatives. (Both challenges were based upon the fact that Negroes did not participate in the election of the delegates and Representatives.)

Although most of the locals are native Mississippians who have always been victimized by segregation and discrimination, I have also placed a number of middle-class students in this category—because of their very practical orientation to black power. The backgrounds of these students are somewhat similar to those of the cosmopolitans, except that the majority come from the South and are perhaps from lower-status families than the cosmopolitans are. These students are deeply involved in attempts to organize black-power programs.

Because of segregation and discrimination, the locals are largely uneducated; they subsist on a totally inadequate income; and they are denied the privileges of first-class citizenship. They have had a lot of experience with the usual forms of harassment and intimidation from local whites. Their entire existence can be perceived in terms of their constant groping for a better way of life. Because of many factors—like their low level of income and education and their Southern, rural, small-town mentality (which to some extent prevents one from acquiring an intellectualized world view)—the definition they have given to black power is a very practical one.

The black-power locals can be considered militants to much the same degree as the cosmopolitans, but on a different level. In essence, the nature and kind of activities in which they are willing to participate (voter registration, running for political office, boycotts, etc.) are indeed militant and are not surpassed by the nature and kind to which the cosmopolitans orient themselves. Indeed, in some cases the locals are deeply involved in realizing black-power programs: In certain counties, women have organized leathercraft and dress-making cooperatives. And in Senator Eastland's home county of Sunflower, an unsuccessful effort was even made to elect an all-black slate of public officials.

The great difference between cosmopolitans and locals is that the locals are committed to concrete economic and political programs, while the cosmopolitans—to varying degrees—endorse such programs but actually have made little effort to realize them.

Most locals perceived black power as a more effective, alternate method of organizing and acquiring those rights they had been seeking. In the past they had been committed to integration. Power had not originally been considered important in and of itself, for it was hoped that America would voluntary give Negroes civil rights. Therefore the locals sought coalition politics—they aligned themselves with Northern labor groups, liberals, national church groups, and so forth. During their several years of involvement, they—like the cosmopolitans—suffered many defeats. For example, many were involved with the Mississippi Summer Project, which brought hundreds of Northerners into the state in 1964. At that time the locals were convinced that such a program would bring about the wide structural changes they desired. But, to their disappointment, once the volunteers returned to the North the old patterns of segregation and discrimination returned. Some of the locals had gone to the Democratic Convention in Atlantic City, N.J., in 1964 hoping to unseat the all-white slate of delegates from Mississippi. When this failed, they invested further moral and physical resources into challenging the legality of the all-white slate of Mississippi Representatives in the U.S. House. Another set-back came when a large contingent pitched their tents on the White House lawn in a last-ditch effort to obtain poverty funds to aid in building adequate housing. All were sharecroppers, evicted because their participation in voter-registration programs was contrary to the desires of their plantation landlords. These evicted sharecroppers later set up residence in the buildings of the inactive Air Force base in Greenville, Miss. They were deeply depressed when officials of the Air Force ordered military police to remove them. One of the leaders of this group remarked, "If the United States Government cares so little about its citizens that it will not allow them to live in its abandoned buildings rather than in unheated tents [this occurred during winter], then that government can't be for real."

I submit that the events outlined above, among many others, caused a large number of the locals—like the cosmopolitans—to pause and question the effectiveness of their traditional organizational tactics and goals. Indeed, many even came to seriously question the Federal Government's sincerity about alleviating the problems of the Negro. A number of the participants in these events stopped being active in the movement. Others began to express strong anti-white sentiments.

Black power was embraced by many of the locals from the very beginning, and they began to reconceptualize their activities within the new framework. To the locals, black power was defined in various ways, some of which follow:

Voter registration is black power. Power is invested in the ballot and that's why the white man worked like hell to keep you away from it. . . . We were even taught that it was not right to register [to vote]. The civil-rights movement in this state started around the issue of voting—we shouldn't forget that.

Black power is political power held by Negroes. It means political control in places where they comprise a majority. . . . Black power is legitimate because any time people are in a majority, they should be able to decide what will and will not happen to them.

Black power was further viewed as a means of combining Negroes into a bond of solidarity. It was seen as a rallying cry, a symbol of identification, and a very concrete tool for action. Many said that former slogans and concepts such as "Freedom Now" were ambiguous. One could easily ask, "Freedom for what and from what?" One local said:

First we wanted Freedom Now. I ran around for six years trying to get my freedom. I really didn't know what it was.

Black power, they felt, was more concrete, for it had as its central thesis the acquisition of power. (Actually, the locals have also defined black power in various ways, and to some the slogan is as ambiguous as "Freedom Now.") The locals felt that Negroes would be able to acquire certain rights only through the control of their economic and political institutions, which—in some cases—also involves the eventual control of the black community. One black-power advocate put it succinctly when he said:

Black power means controlling the Negro community. It means that if the Negro community doesn't want white cops coming in, they can't come in. It means political, economic, and social control.

Asked how this control could be obtained, he replied:

We will have to start putting our money together to organize cooperatives, and other kinds of businesses. We can get political power by putting Negroes into public offices. . . . We will have to tell them to vote only for Negro candidates.

To others, control over the black community was not the goal, but rather a *share* in the existing power:

All we're saying to the white man is we want some power. Black power is just plain power. . . . It just means that Negroes are tired of being without power and want to share in it.

Thus, we can observe that there are several variations of the concept, all revolving around a central theme: the acquisition of power by Negroes for their own use, both offensively and defensively.

Despite the obvious practical orientation of the locals, there can also be found traces of black consciousness and black nationalism in their thought patterns. Most have never read Garvy, Fanon, Malcolm X, and other nationalists, but they tend to readily identify with the content of speeches made by Stokely Carmichael bearing the message of black nationalism. They are prone to agree with the cosmopolitans who speak to them about ridding themselves of their "oppressors." When the chairman of the Mississippi Freedom Democratic Party speaks of overthrowing neo-colonialism in Mississippi, shouts of "Amen!" can be heard from the audience. There is also a tendency in this group to oppose the current war in Vietnam on the grounds that America should first concentrate on liberating Negroes within the United States' borders. The locals also believe that the war is indeed an unjust one. Perhaps the following statement is typical:

Black men have been stripped of everything. If it takes plack power to do something about this, let us have it. Black power has got the country moving and white people don't like it. We marched into Dominica, we marched into Vietnam. Now if we [black people] can conquer this country, we will conquer the world.

There is a growing feeling among both locals and cosmopolitans of kinship with the colored peoples of the world, including the Vietnamese. To engage in warfare against other colored people is regarded as a contradiction of this bond of solidarity.

For both the Mississippi cosmopolitans and locals, then, it was mainly frustration that drew them to the concept of black power.

The black-power slogan should be viewed in the perspective of the overall civil-rights movement, one of the most popular social movements in the history of this country. Now, there are some scholars who maintain that, by viewing a particular social movement over a period of time, one can discern a typical sequence: the movement's crystallization of social unrest; its phase of active agitation and proselytism; its organized phase; and the achievement of its objectives. The civil-rights movement, with much success, achieved each of these phases—except the final one, the achievement of objectives. Despite the great amount of effort and resources expended by black people and their allies to obtain civil rights, there was a disproportionate lack of gains. Indeed, in much of Mississippi and the South, conditions have barely changed from 10 or even 20 years ago. Many black people are still earning their livelihood from sharecropping and tenant farming; many household heads are still unable to earn more than $500 a year; many black children are still deprived of adequate education because of the lack of facilities and adequately trained teachers. To date, only 42.1 percent of Negroes of voting age are registered as opposed to 78.9 percent of whites. We still hear of lynchings and other forms of violence of which Negroes are the victims.

The black-power thrust is thus an inevitable outgrowth of the disillusionment that black people have experienced in their intense efforts to become integrated into the mainstream of American society. Thwarted by traditional formulas and organizational restrictions, some Mississippi Negroes have responded to the black-power concept in a sometimes semirational, emotionally charged manner—because it seemed the only available resource with which they could confront white American society.

How was the black-power concept related to the expulsion of whites from leadership positions in the movement? The fact is that the alienation and disaffection found throughout the entire black-power group also resulted from strained interpersonal relations with white civil-rights workers. During the past two years, there has been a growing belief among black people in Mississippi that white civil-rights workers should go into the *white* communities of that state to work. Only then, they contended, could the "inherent racism" in American society, with particular reference to the "Southern racist," begin to be dealt with. Even the seriousness of white civil-rights workers was questioned. Many Negroes felt that a sizable number of them had come South mainly to resolve their very personal emotional difficulties, and not to help impoverished black Mississippians. Rather, they were considered rebellious youth who wanted only to act out their rebellion in the most unconventional ways. Stokely Carmichael stated:

Too many young, middle-class Americans, like some sort of Pepsi generation, have wanted to come alive through the black community; they've wanted to be where the action was—and the action has been in the black community. . . .

It's important to note that those white people who feel alienated from white society and run into the black society are incapable of confronting the white society with its racism where it really does exist.

Much strain also resulted from the inability of many black civil-rights activists—skilled organizers but lacking the formal education and other technical skills white workers possessed—to deal with the increased bureaucratization of the civil-rights movement (writing proposals for foundation grants, for example). Black activists, in addition, constantly complained about the focus of the mass media on white "all-American" volunteers who had come South to work in the movement. The media never paid attention to the thousands of black people who frequently took far greater risks. These factors played a major role in destroying the bond of solidarity that had once existed between whites and blacks in the movement. Before the emergence of the black-power concept, it is true, many young black civil-rights workers had cast white civil-rights workers in the same category as all other white people. The new slogan was, to some extent, a form of justification for their own prejudice against whites.

In terms of practical considerations, however, urging the white volunteers to leave the black communities has had negative effects. SNCC and CORE, which at one time directed most of the grass-roots organizing, have always depended upon the economic and volunteer resources of liberal white individuals and groups. These resources are scarce nowadays.

On another level, there have been positive results from removing whites from black communities. Black activists—all cosmopolitans and some locals—contend that, now that the whites have gone, they feel more self-confident and capable of running their own programs. They tend to view the earlier period of the movement, when whites played active roles in executing the programs, as having been a necessary phase; but they maintain that the time has arrived when black people must launch and execute their own programs.

Clearly, the long-range aims of the locals and cosmopolitans are basically the same. Unlike Negroes in such traditional organizations as the N.A.A.C.P., locals and cosmopolitans have turned away from integration. Both groups want to unite black people and build political, economic, and social institutions that will render a certain amount of control to the black community. For some time, however, the two groups have been operating on different levels. The cosmopolitans focus on developing black consciousness among black people, which they consider a necessary step to developing black power; the locals concentrate on solving the immediate problems resulting from segregation and discrimination.

While it may seem that the locals are more prudent and realistic than the cosmopolitans, it should be said that there are many positive features to black nationalism and black consciousness. It *is* important to establish a positive black identity in a great many sectors of the black communities, both North and South, rural and urban, lower and middle class. Indeed, it is both important and legitimate to teach black people (or any other ethnic minority) about their history, placing special emphasis upon the positive contributions of other black people. Thus black consciousness has the potential to create unity and solidarity among black people and to give them hope and self-confidence. Perhaps it fulfills certain needs in black people that society, on the whole, cannot. Martin Luther King has made the following statement about black consciousness:

One must not overlook the positive value in calling the Negro to a new sense of manhood, to a deep feeling of racial pride and to an audacious appreciation of his heritage. The Negro must be grasped by a new realization of his dignity and worth. He must stand up amid a system that still oppresses him and develop an unassailable and majestic sense of his own value. *He must no longer be ashamed of being black.* (Emphasis mine.)

Moreover, the task of getting blacks to act *as blacks, by* themselves and *for* themselves, is necessary for developing black consciousness, or psychological equality. Thus one is led to the conclusion that black consciousness does *necessarily* call for the expulsion of whites from leadership roles in the black communities.

The locals, on the other hand, have adopted concrete strategies that, in reality, involve the same kind of techniques that existed in the integration era. Specifically, when they refer to developing black-power programs, they speak of registering to vote, running for political office, and building independent political parties. As for the economic situation, they have begun to concentrate on building cooperatives and small businesses, and on almost-exclusively patronizing black merchants in an effort to "keep the money in the black community." If we turn back two years, however, we find that the same strategies, though somewhat modified, were being used then. In the past, the locals concentrated on registering large numbers of black people to vote, in an effort to be able to have a voice in the decision-making apparatus. The emphasis is now on registering to vote so that the Negro can have control over his community and eventual control over his political destiny. Cooperatives were organized at least a year before the black-power concept emerged, but—ever since emphasis was put on economic control—there has been an expansion and intensification in certain sectors of this area. At present, cooperatives are still operating on a small-scale, though, considering the masses of people whose lives could be immensely improved by cooperatives.

The differences in the emphasis on priorities of achieving black power between locals and cosmopolitans can be viewed as complementary rather than oppositional, because each level of emphasis is vital for the achievement of their goals. This is becoming increasingly true since, within the last year, black-power advocates have taken a far more aggressive and militant stance toward the realization of such aims. Locals who a year ago might have questioned the importance and feasibility of "Black Liberation" schools, which teach black history and culture, are less likely to do so now. This is an indication that there is a trend toward unity between the groups. Because of the strong emphasis among some sectors of the black-power movement on drawing the parallels of the plight of black Americans with that of the inhabitants of the Third World, locals are quite likely to become more cosmopolitan through time.

Through the development of such unity, there is a great possibility that black-power advocates in Mississippi will again turn to creative, large-scale organizing that would incorporate the major emphases of each group: black consciousness and immediate gains.

The key question, of course, is, what are the prospects for Mississippi Negroes' developing black-power institutions in the near future? Clearly, this will depend to a great extent upon the number of organizers in the field, on adequate economic resources, and on commitments from major civil-rights organizations to the Mississippi scene. Certainly the presence of a local charismatic leader also would aid in the development of pervasive black-power institutions. Indeed, a black-power "prophet" whose task was to keep the message before all the advocates would give them immeasurable support and strength for their undertakings.

Where black-power institutions have a good chance of developing at present are in the small number of Mississippi counties where there are strong black-power organizations with large Negro voting populations. Since the cosmopolitans are reentering the field and beginning to organize (and some of the most skilled organizers are in this group), the prospects—here at least—seem favorable. On the other hand, it seems highly doubtful at this point that the needed resources can be obtained from the traditional sources (Northern students, white liberals, church and labor organizations). So these resources (inadequate as they may be) may have to be obtained from the black community. CORE and SNCC have already begun to establish financial bases in the black communities throughout the country. Should this tactic fail, perhaps there will be a revaluation of the strategies employed in the acquisition of black power.

November 1967

FURTHER READING SUGGESTED BY THE AUTHOR:

The Wretched of the Earth by Franz Fanon (New York: Grove Press, 1963). The role of violence in a revolutionary movement and the catharsis it gives the oppressed.

Where Do We Go From Here: Chaos or Community? by Martin Luther King (New York: Harper and Row, 1967). King analyzes past gains of the civil-rights movement and suggests further activities, all nonviolent.

Social Theory and Social Structure by Robert K. Merton (Glencoe, Ill.: The Free Press, 1963). See "Patterns of Influence: Locals and Cosmopolitans," an elaboration of the typologies used in this article.

White Reflections on Black Power by Charles E. Fager (Grand Rapids, Mich.: William B. Eerdmans Publishing Co., 1967). Fager argues that black people are justified in calling for black nationalism and black power. He suggests that white liberals continue to support the movement, but only when called upon, and that they withdraw from leadership roles to allow blacks to assert themselves as leaders.

Some Reservations About Black Power

DAVID RIESMAN

My own experience with the Deep South has been almost entirely vicarious, and my reflections on Joyce Ladner's discerning observations are set forth in a spirit of tentativeness and questioning.

The psychiatrist Robert J. Lifton, discussing the dissident attitudes of young Japanese students, distinguishes two non-accommodative attitudes, which he calls *Restorationist* and *Transformationist*. The Restorationist looks back to an earlier, more pastoral epoch and wants to radically re-arrange and, if necessary, destroy contemporary society in the name of the past. The Transformationist, on the other hand, rejects the past as well as the present. Both styles give their possessors a way of interpreting their despair and frustration, as well as some sort of quasi-political, quasi-mystical agenda to cope with these feelings. When I was in Japan in 1961, I met some of the leaders of the *Zengakuren*, the federation of Japanese students. With

155

their grandiose talk, they seemed much less pragmatic than comparable American student activists were at that time.

Today I am not so sure, because some American students, particularly whites who are devotees of black power, often remind me of the *Zengakuren*. Negro and white cosmopolitans in the civil-rights movement have a kind of nostalgia that leads them to believe that American society is now more corrupt, and perhaps even more racist, than it ever was. The war in Vietnam and white ethnic hostility in Cicero are viewed as part of an overall pattern so rotten and menacing that, as Fanon believed of the Algerian victims of colonialism, only violence by the oppressed can be therapeutic.

My own impression is somewhat different. It seems to me that conditions have changed considerably for the better during the last 10 or 20 years, even in the Deep South. The frustration and despair that Miss Ladner finds in the cosmopolitans seems to me essentially to reflect their disappointment that things are not getting better *fast* enough. This frustration and despair also seems to be the source of their assumption that American society and all whites are inherently racist, for this assumption protects them from ever again experiencing either illusion or betrayal. But this assumption is a simplification of life, and as a remedy for the ambiguities of existence I find it understandable but sad. Thus even Martin Luther King Jr. declares that his people feel American society "has become corrupt" and that the Establishment (whatever that is) is worse than it once was.

No doubt, for many Southern Negroes come North, the past *was* more secure and definitive: As they often say, you knew where you stood. For peasants forced out of sharecropper existence into urban ghettos, with no preparation for urban life, the present could in some sense be worse—more alive and free, but also more disorganized and threatening. For Northern Negro cosmopolitans come South, white violence and the omnipresent white hostility and condescension also provide a shock. It may well be that there *are* parts of the South where things have gotten absolutely, rather than relatively, worse. But, contrary to the cosmopolitan impression Miss Ladner accepts, and despite the deprivations, lynchings, and other violence, the relative opening-up of some aspects of Deep South life seems to me, as it does to many fearsome and threatened local whites, undeniable and almost certainly irreversible. This spring I read the local press and corresponded with students and faculty at a number of Southern Negro colleges where there have been demonstrations and protests. And I doubt if 10 or 20 years ago the students who boycotted classes at the State College in Orangeburg, S.C., would have been so certain that the white racists would not close the college down. Indeed, these students actually succeeded in ousting the college president—in a new squeeze between the considerably-more-tolerant white community and the much-less-tolerant Negroes

This last example suggests a theme implicit in Miss Ladner's paper, namely, the elements of class as well as of racial hostility that are involved in some uses of the black-power concept. (I do not mean to suggest that class is more important than race, but only that it is largely covert and ancillary.) When the lower-class locals, or some of them, accept the ideological leadership of the migrating cosmopolitans, it has meant that the local, "established," middle-class Negro leadership has been ousted. The rejection of the whites, which Miss Ladner's paper describes, also has elements of class as well as racial conflict, since the whites are almost invariably from upper-class or upper-middle-class backgrounds.

However, if the whites are driven out physically, under the slogan of black power, does this mean that they are spiritually rejected also? We might ask whether girls in women's colleges think less about men than girls in coed colleges. The cosmopolitans at least have had contact with whites, and the white world inevitably presses its reminders on them. (The very fact that we whites talk constantly about black power, could, I am inclined to think, be felt by black-power advocates as an intrusion, as a mild kind of intellectual imperialism—hardly less so when ardent but nevertheless presently-excluded white fellow-travelers praise black power.) The locals, with far less personal experience and contact with whites, may—in the physical absence of the whites—become even shakier in their self-esteem, wavering between feelings of abasement and of grandiosity, outcomes that are all the more likely because, as Miss Ladner notes with great penetration, the slogan "black power" only *seems* more concrete than the slogan "Freedom Now" (which the black-power advocates see as soft, vague, hortatory, and inchoate). In fact, the black militants are often captives of the very whites they reject because, by this total rejection, they must do what the whites do *not* do, or vice versa, and they are in the position of other reactive nationalisms, whether in Israel or Ireland

Lacking, as many have pointed out, a territorial base, the advocates of black power are in an even more difficult position than the advocates of other reactive nationalisms. In the absence of a clear program, it will not be easy for them to point to concrete communal organizations as models, either in the economy or on the land. Where there *is* a territorial base, as in some Mississippi counties or in the ghettos, the black-power advocates may discover that by eliminating whites they may succeed in only subjecting themselves to new black despotisms. They may eliminate white policemen from the ghettos only to place themselves under the domination of the most violent Negroes at loose in the ghettos. Black militant students, in combination with college-administration reactionaries, may squeeze white teaching interns out of a Negro college—and yet this may not result in liberation. Many of the upper-class and middle-class Negro students, the cosmopolitans, made extraordinary sacrifices in the early years of the movement, and many could be leaders on their college campuses—because they are intellectually and academically, as well as organizationally, talented. In the present mood, however, the cosmopolitans both wish to and are forced to share mass racial attitudes, at least rhetorically, because the Negro lower class is alleged to be more truly "Negro." Their devotion to the cause of racial solidarity may, for a time, minimize the extent of class conflict within the Negro community, but the cosmopolitans may not always escape being the target of such conflict.

In contrast, the Black Muslim appears to be attempting to transform himself in the process of building a more patriarchal, more hierarchical, more sober, less self-indulgent community. Some of the cosmopolitans are no less sober, but they do not accept the Muslim disciplines; and some who listen to the Muslim slogans, and no more, may gain an all-too-precarious dignity and self-confidence, shored up with invective, a vague sense of allies in the Third World, and a hair style that in some cases can be spectacularly handsome.

Perhaps it is my want of imagination, but I find a community of the dispossessed hard to envisage without charismatic leaders, major organizing drives, and fuller resources. Consider in this connection the interpretations that both locals and cosmopolitans have put on their defeats in Mississippi. They began with the erroneous assumption that if all Negroes were registered to vote, they could somehow be a majority. But they are not, even in Mississippi. And a few local electoral victories scarcely assuage despair. Similarly, the accomplishments—in the face of terrible obstacles—of the Child Development Group of Mississippi (brought about, to be sure, with the support of white churches and a modicum of Federal Government leverage) seem more like total failure than limited success.

In these situations, excessive hopes inevitably lead to extravagant despair. I am reminded of the deep frustration of peasant communities, which—if their momentum is to be kept up—cannot endure a single defeat or even a delay in the course of a string of victories and advances. The disciplined Marxist's willingness to wait for victory is virtually absent; the present need is for "action," at least as occupational therapy. This leads to charisma without an object, to revolutionary tactics without a revolutionary situation, to revolutionary rhetoric that may in turn bring about a new and even deeper cynicism and nihilism.

In an article in *Daedalus* devoted to the Negro in America, James Tobin observes that the balance of payments and de Gaulle's attitude toward it and toward gold may be more important for the Negro American than anything happening autonomously within the Negro community or among its immediate white allies or enemies. A guaranteed annual income, or a negative income tax, might do more to keep Negroes on subsistence farms in the South or in Southern towns, preventing the dispossessed from being forced into the cities or into tent communities, than anything black power can do on its own. No doubt, this is too economistic a view, and leaves aside the immediate question of self-respect vs. powerlessness that is vital for leadership, cohesion, even sanity.

In its integrative aspect, the concept of black power is

helping to reshape Negro self-definitions, whether of beauty or success or outlook, so that (for example) in *Ebony* magazine there are often interesting contradictions between the increasingly militant articles and the still conventional advertising beamed at Negroes upwardly mobile in the white tradition. And where Negroes do live contiguously, they may in the course of time develop—beyond the churches and the lodges and the college fraternities—a growing network of self-help organizations for which concepts of black power (like those of *négritude* in French West Africa) may serve as a partial mystique. Yet it also seems true that no mystique suffices to short-cut the grave problems of economic and cultural development, either in the Third World or here at home, whatever precarious support it provides for the pride of the oppressed.

November 1967

The Significance of Soul

ULF HANNERZ

In the black ghettos of the large cities of the northern United States, the last few years have witnessed the emergence of the concept of "soul." For instance, in every riot from Watts to Washington, hastily printed signs were rushed to doors and windows of Negro-owned businesses, all carrying the same message: Soul Brother. These businesses were usually spared. Perhaps this is why the term cropped up in a cartoon during the Washington riots —the cartoon showed a "Soul Brother" sign on the iron fence surrounding the White House.

Recently, while doing field work in a lower-class Negro area in Washington, D.C., I considered soul from the standpoint of its social significance in Negro slums in Northern American cities. The neighborhood's inhabitants share the characteristics of America's lower-class urban poor: a high rate of unemployment; a considerable amount of crime (including juvenile delinquency); and a great many households headed by adult women, while the men are either absent or only temporarily attached to the family.

Of the people at the field site, a minority were born in Washington, D.C. The majority are emigrants from the South, particularly from Virginia, North Carolina, and South Carolina. Apart from conducting field work in this area by means of traditional participant observation, I also paid attention to those impersonal media that are specifically intended for a lower-class Negro audience: radio stations (three in Washington were clearly aimed at Negroes); the recording industry; and stage shows featuring Negro rock and roll artists and comedians. (The phrase "rhythm and blues" used by whites to denote Negro rock and roll is not widely used by the Negroes themselves.) These media have played a prominent part in promoting the vocabulary of soul. On the other hand, both the local Negro press, such as the Washington *Afro-American,* and the national Negro publications, like the monthly *Ebony,* are largely middle-class-oriented and thus of limited value for understanding life in the ghetto.

What, then, is soul? As the concept has come to be used in urban ghettos, it stands for "the essence of Negroness." And, it should be added, this "Negroness" refers to the kind of Negro with which the urban slum-dweller is most familar—people like himself. The question whether a middle-class, white-collar, suburban Negro also has soul is often met with consternation. In fact, soul seems to be a folk conception of the lower-class urban Negro's own "national character." Modes of action, personal attributes, and certain artifacts are given the soul label. In conversations one typically hears statements such as "Man, he got a lot of soul." This appreciative opinion may be given concerning anybody in the ghetto, but more often by younger adults or adolescents about their peers. Soul talk is particularly common among younger men. This sex differentiation in the use of soul may be quite important in understanding the basis of the soul concept.

The choice of the term "soul" for this "Negroness" is in itself noteworthy. First of all, it shows the influence of religion on lower-class Negroes, even those who are not themselves active church members. Expressions of religious derivation—such as "God, have mercy!"—are frequent in everyday speech among all lower-class Negroes, in all contexts. A very great number of people, of course, have been regular churchgoers at some point, at least at the time they attended Sunday school, and many are involved in church activities—perhaps in one of the large Baptist churches, but more often in small spiritualist storefront churches. Although the people who use the soul vocabulary are seldom regular churchgoers themselves, they have certainly been fully (although sometimes indirectly) exposed to the religious idiom of "soul-stirring" revival meetings.

Further, the choice of soul (a term that in church usage means "the essentially human") to refer to "the essentially Negro," as the new concept of soul does, certainly has strong implications of race pride. If soul is Negro, the non-Negro is non-soul, and, in a unique turnabout, somewhat less human. Although I have never heard such a point of view spelled out, it seems to be implicitly accepted as part of soul ideology. What is soul is not only different from what is not soul (particularly what is mainstream, middle-class American); it is also superior. The term "soul" appraises as well as describes. If one asks a young man what a soul brother is, the answer is usually something like "Someone who's hip, someone who knows what he's doing." It may be added here that although both soul brother and soul sister are used for soul personified, the former is more common. Like soul, soul brother and soul sister are terms used particularly by younger men.

Let us now note a few fields that are particularly soulful. One is music (where the concept may have originated), especially progressive jazz and rock and roll. James Brown, a leading rock and roll singer, is often referred to as "Soul Brother Number One"; two of the largest record stores in Washington, with almost exclusively Negro customers, are the "Soul Shack" and the "Soul City." Recently a new magazine named *Soul* appeared; its main outlet seems to be these de facto segregated record stores. It contains stories on rock and roll artists, disc jockeys, and so on. Excellence in musical expression is indeed a part of the lower-class Negro's self-conception, and white rock and roll is often viewed with scorn as a poor imitation of the Negro genius. Resentment is often aimed at the Beatles, who stand as typical of white intrusion into a Negro field. (Occasionally a Beatles melody has become a hit in the Negro ghetto as well, but only when performed in a local version by a Negro group, such as the recording of "Day Tripper" by the Vontastics. In such a case, there is little or no mention of the melody's Beatles origin.)

The commercial side of Negro entertainment is, of course, directly tied to soul music. The Howard Theater in Washington, with counterparts in other large Negro ghettos in the United States, stages shows of touring rock and roll groups and individual performers. Each show usually runs a week, with four or five performances every day. Larger shows also make one-night appearances at the Washington Coliseum. Occasionally, a comedian takes part; Moms Mabley, Pigmeat Markham, and Red Foxx are among those who draw large, predominantly Negro audiences.

The emcees of these shows are often celebrities in their own right. Some, such as "King" Coleman and "Georgeous"

George, tour regularly with the shows, and others are local disc jockeys from the white-owned Negro radio stations. In Washington, such disc jockeys as "The Nighthawk," Bob Terry of the WOL "Soul Brothers," and "Soulfinger," Fred Correy of the WOOK "Soul Men," make highly appreciated appearances at the Howard. It is clear that the commercial establishments with a vested interest in a separate Negro audience have latched onto the soul vocabulary, using it to further their own interests as well to support its use among the audience. Thus there is also, for instance, a WWRL "soul brother radio" in New York. But the soul vocabulary is not just a commercial creation. It existed before it was commercialized, and the fact that it seems so profitable for commercial establishments to fly the banner of soul indicates that, whatever part these establishments have had in promoting soul, it has fallen into already fertile ground.

A second area of widespread soul symbolism is food. The dishes that Negroes now call soul food they once called "Southern cooking" and still do to some extent; but in the Northern ghettos these foods increasingly come to stand for race rather than region. In the center of the Washington Negro area, for instance, the Little Harlem Restaurant advertises "soul food." There are a number of such foods: chitlins, hog maw, black-eyed peas, collard greens, corn bread, and grits. Typically, they were the poor man's food in the rural South. In the urban North, they may still be so to some degree, but in the face of the diversity of the urban environment they also come to stand as signs of ethnicity. References to soul food occur frequently in soul music—two of the hits of the winter 1966-67 were "Grits and Cornbread" by the Soul Runners and the Joe Cuba Sextet's "Bang! Bang!," with the refrain "corn bread, hog maw, and chitlin." Sometimes the names of soul foods may themselves be used as more or less synonymous with soul—Negro entertainers on stage, talking of their experiences while journeying between ghetto shows around the country, sometimes refer to it as "the chitlin circuit," and this figure of speech usually draws much favorable audience reaction.

What, then, is "soul" about soul music and soul food? It may be wise to be cautious here, since there is little intellectualizing and analyzing on the part of the ghetto's inhabitants on this subject. I believe that this comparative absence of defining may itself be significant, and I will return to this later. Here, I will only point to a few basic characteristics of soul that I feel make it "essentially Negro" —referring again, of course, to urban lower-class Negroes.

There is, of course, the Southern origin. The "Down Home" connotations are particularly attached to soul food; but while Negro music has changed more, and commercial rock and roll is an urban phenomenon, this music is certainly seen as the latest stage of an unfolding heritage. Thus the things that are soul, while taking on new significance in the urban environment, provide some common historical tradition for ghetto inhabitants. One might also speculate that the early and, from then on, constant and intimate exposure to these foods and to this music—radios and record players seem to belong to practically every ghetto home—may make them appear particularly basic to a "Negro way of life."

When it comes to soul music, there are a couple of themes in style and content that I would suggest are pervasive in ghetto life, and are probably very close to the everyday experience of ghetto inhabitants.

One of these is lack of control over the environment. There is a very frequent attitude among soul brothers that one's environment is somewhat like a jungle, where tough, smart people may survive and where a lot happens to make it worthwhile and enjoyable just to "watch the scene"—if one does not have too high hopes of controlling it. Many of the reactions to listening to progressive jazz seem connected with this view: "Oooh, man, there just ain't nothing you can do about it but sit there and feel it goin' all the way into you." Without being able to do much about proving it, I feel that experiences—desirable or undesirable —in which one can only passively perceive what is happening are an essential fact of ghetto life, for better or for worse; thus it is soul.

Related to this theme are unstable personal relationships, in particular between the sexes. It is well known that among lower-class urban Negroes there are many "broken" families (households without a husband and father), many temporary common-law unions, and in general relatively little consensus on sex roles. It is not much of an exaggeration, then, to speak of a constant battle of the sexes. Indeed, success with the opposite sex is a focal concern in lower-class Negro life. From this area come most of the lyrics of contemporary rock and roll music. (It may be objected that this is true of white rock and roll as well; but this is very much to the point. For white rock and roll is predominantly adolescent music, and reaches people who also have unstable personal relationships. In the case of lower-class urban Negroes, such relationships are characteristic of a much wider age-range, and music on this theme also reaches this wider range.) Some titles of recent rock and roll hits may show this theme: "I'm Losing You" (Temptations), "Are You Lonely" (Freddy Scott), "Yours Until Tomorrow" (Dee Dee Warwick), "Keep Me Hangin' On" (Supremes). Thus soul may also stand for a bittersweet experience that arises from contacts with the other sex (although there are certainly other sources). This bittersweetness, of course, was already typical of the blues.

Turning to style, a common element in everyday social interaction—as well as among storefront-church preachers, Negro comedians, and rock and roll singers—is an alternation between aggressive, somewhat boastful behavior and plaintive behavior from an implicit underdog position. This style occurs in many situations and may itself be related to the unstable personal relationships mentioned above. In any case, it seems that this style is seen as having soul; without describing its elements, soul brothers tend to describe its occurrences in varying contexts as "soulful."

I have hesitated to try to analyze and define soul, because what seems to be important in the emergence of the present soul concept is the fact that there is *something* that is felt to be soul; *what* that something is isn't so important. There is, of course, some logic to this. If soul is what is "essentially Negro," it should not be necessary for soul brothers to spend much time analyzing it. Asking about soul, one often receives answers such as, "You know, we don't talk much about it, but we've all been through it, so we know what it is anyway." Probably this is to some extent true. What the lack of a clear definition points to is that soul vocabulary is predominantly for the in-crowd. It is a symbol of solidarity among the people of the ghetto —but not in more than a weak and implicit sense of solidarity *against* anybody else. Soul is turned inward; and so everybody who is touched by it is supposed to know what it means.

The few interpreters of soul to the outside world are, in fact, outsiders. LeRoi Jones, the author, is a convert to ghetto life who, like so many converts, seems to have become more militantly partisan than the authentic ghetto inhabitants. Originally he rather impartially noted the ethnocentric bias of soul:

" . . . the soul brother means to recast the social order

in his own image. White is then not 'right,' as the old blues had it, but a liability, since the culture of white precludes the possession of the Negro 'soul.' "

Now he preaches the complete destruction of American society, an activist program that I am sure is far out of step with the immediate concerns of the average soul brother. Lerone Bennett, an editor of the middle-class *Ebony* magazine, is not particularly interested in what he calls "the folk myth of soul," yet he explains what he feels soul really is:

" . . . the American counterpart of the African concept of Negritude, a distinct quality of Negroness growing out of the Negro's experience and not his genes. . . . Soul is the Negro's antithesis to America's thesis (white), a confrontation of spirits that could and should lead to a higher synthesis of the two."

I am not convinced that Bennett's conception is entirely correct; it is certainly not expressed in the idiom of the ghetto. Charles Keil, an ethomusicologist, probably comes closer to the folk conception than anyone else—by giving what amounts to a catalogue of those ghetto values and experiences that the inhabitants recognize as their own:

"The breath of life"; "It don't mean a thing if you ain't got that swing"; "Grits and greens"; and so on.

In doing so, of course, one does not get a short and comprehensive definition of soul that is acceptable to all and in every situation—one merely lists the fields in which a vocabulary of soul is particularly likely to be expressed.

The vocabulary of soul, then, is a relatively recent phenomenon, and it is used among younger Negro ghetto dwellers, particularly young men, to designate in a highly approving manner the experiences and characteristics that are "essentially Negro." As such, it is employed within the group, although it is clear that by discussing what is "typically Negro" one makes an implicit reference to non-Negro society. Now, why has such a vocabulary emerged in this group at just this point of Negro history?

For a long time, the social boundaries that barred Negro Americans from educational and economic achievements have been highly impermeable. Although lower-class Negroes largely accepted the values of mainstream American culture, the obvious impermeability of social boundaries has probably prevented a more complete commitment on their part to the achievement of those goals that have been out of reach. Instead, there has been an adjustment to the lower-class situation, in which goals and values more appropriate to the ascribed social position of the group have been added to, and to some extent substituted for, the mainstream norms. The style of life of the lower class, in this case the Negro lower class, is different from that of the upper classes, and the impermeability of group boundaries and the unequal distribution of resources have long kept the behavioral characteristics of the groups relatively stable and distinct from each other. However, to a great extent, one of the groups—the lower-class Negroes—would have preferred the style of life of the other group—the middle-class whites—had it been available to them.

Lower-class Negroes have only been able to do the best they could with what they have had. They have had two cultures—the mainstream culture they are relatively familiar with, which is in many ways apparently superior and preferable and which has been closed to them, and the ghetto culture, which is a second choice and is based on the circumstances of the ascribed social position.

This, of course, sounds to some extent like the position of what has often been described as that of "the marginal man." Such a position may cause psychological problems. But when the position is very clearly defined and where the same situation is shared by many, it is perhaps reasonably acceptable. There is a perfectly understandable reason for one's failure to reach one's goal. Nobody of one's own kind is allowed to reach that goal, and the basis of the condition is a social rule rather than a personal failure. There are indications that marginality is more severely felt if the barrier is not absolute—if crossing a boundary, although uncertain, is possible. According to Alan C. Kerckhoff and Thomas C. McCormick,

" . . . an absolute barrier between the two groups is less conducive to personality problems than 'grudging, uncertain, and unpredictable acceptance.' The impact of the rejection on an individual's personality organization will depend to some extent upon the usual treatment accorded members of his group by the dominant group. If his group as a whole faces a rather permeable barrier and he meets with more serious rejection, the effect on him is likely to be more severe than the same treatment received by a more thoroughly rejected group (one facing an impermeable barrier)."

Recent changes in race relations in the United States have indeed made the social barriers to achievement seem less impermeable to the ghetto population. One often hears people in the ghetto expressing opinions such as, "Yeah, there are so many programs, job-training and things, going on, man, so if you got anything on the ball you can make it." On the other hand, there are also assertions about the impossibility of getting anywhere. Obviously, a clear-cut exclusion from mainstream American culture is gradually being replaced by ambivalence about one's actual chances. This ambivalence, of course, seems to represent an accurate estimate of the situation: The lower-class Negro continues to be disadvantaged, but his chances of moving up and out of the ghetto are probably improving.

People do indeed trickle out of the ghetto.

It is in this situation that the vocabulary of soul has emerged. It is a response, I feel, to the uncertainty of the ghetto dweller's situation. This uncertainty is particularly strong for the younger male, the soul brother. While women have always been able to live closer to mainstream culture norms, as homemakers and possibly with a job keeping them in touch with the middle-class world, men have had less chance to practice and become competent in mainstream culture. Older men tend to feel that current social changes come too late for them, but they have higher expectations for the following generation. Therefore, the present generation of young men in the Negro ghettos of the United States is placed in a new situation, to which they are making new responses, and much of the unrest in the ghettos today is perhaps the result of these emerging pressures.

This new situation must be taken into account if we are to understand the emergence of the soul vocabulary. The increasing ambivalence about one's opportunities in the changing social structure may be accompanied by doubts about one's own worth. Earlier, the gap between mainstream culture norms and the lower-class Negro's achievements could be explained easily, by referring to social barriers. Today, the suspicion arises that under-achievement is due to one's own failure, and self-doubt may result.

Such self-doubt can be reduced in different ways. Some young men, of course, are able to live up to mainstream norms of achievement, thereby reducing the strain on themselves (but at the same time increasing the strain on the others). Higher self-esteem can also be obtained by affirming that the boundaries are still impermeable. A third possibility is to set new standards for achievement, proclaiming one's own achievements to be the ideals. It is not necessary, of course, that the same way of reducing self-doubt always be applied. In the case of soul, the method is that of idealizing one's own achievements, proclaiming one's own way of life to be superior. Yet the same soul brother may argue at other times that he is what he is because he is not allowed to become anything else.

In any case, soul is by native public definition superior, and the motive of the soul vocabulary, I believe, is above all to reduce self-doubt by persuading soul brothers that they are successful. Being a soul brother is belonging to a select group instead of to a residual category of people who have not succeeded. Thus, the soul vocabulary is a device of rhetoric. By talking about people who have soul, about soul music and about soul food, the soul brother attempts to establish himself in the role of an expert and connoisseur; by talking to others of his group in these terms, he identifies with them and confers the same role on them. Using soul rhetoric is a way of convincing others of one's own worth and of their worth. As Kenneth Burke expresses it,

> "A man can be his own audience, insofar as he, even in his secret thoughts, cultivates certain ideas or images for the effect he hopes they may have upon him; he is here what Mead would call 'an "I" addressing its "me" '; and in this respect he is being rhetorical quite as though he were using pleasant imagery to influence an outside audience rather than one within."

The soul vocabulary has thus emerged from the social basis of a number of individuals, in effective interaction with one another, with similar problems of adjustment to a new situation. The use of soul rhetoric is a way of meeting their needs as long as it occurs in situations where they can mutually support each other. Here, of course, is a clue to the confinement of the rhetoric to in-group situations.

If soul talk were directed toward outsiders, they might not accept the claims of its excellence—it is not *their* "folk myth." Viewing soul as such a device of rhetoric, it is also easier to understand why the soul brothers do not want it made the topic of too much intellectualizing. As Clifford Geertz has made clear, by analyzing and defining an activity one achieves maximum intellectual clarity at the expense of emotional commitment. It is doubtful that soul rhetoric would thrive on too much intellectual clarity; rather, by expressing soul ideals in a circumspect manner—in terms of emotionally charged symbols such as soul food and soul music—one can avoid the rather sordid realities underlying these emotions. As I pointed out already, the shared lower-class Negro experiences that seem to be the bases of soul are hardly such as to bring out a surge of ethnic pride. That is the psychological reason for keeping the soul concept diffuse.

There is also, I believe, a sociological basis for the diffuseness. The more exactly a soul brother would define soul, the fewer others would probably agree upon the "essential Negroness" of his definition; and, as we have seen, a basic idea of the rhetoric of soul is to cast others into roles that satisfy them and at the same time support one's own position. If people are cast into a role of soul brother and then find that there has been a definition established for that role that they cannot accept, the result may be overt disagreement and denial of solidarity, rather than mutual deference. As it is, soul can be an umbrella concept for a rather wide variety of definitions of one's situation, and the soul brothers who are most in need of the race-centered conception can occasionally get at least fleeting allegiance to soul from others with whom, in reality, they share relatively little—for instance, individuals who are clearly upwardly mobile. Once I listened to a long conversation about soul music in a rather heterogeneous group of young Negro men, who all agreed on the soulfulness of the singers whose records they were playing. Afterwards I asked one of the men, who was clearly upwardly mobile, about his conception of soul. He answered that soul is earthy, that "There is nothing specifically Negro about it." Yet the very individuals with whom he had just agreed on matters of soul had earlier given me the opposite answer—only Negroes have soul. Thus, by avoiding definitions, they had found together an area of agreement and satisfaction in soul by merely assuming that there was a shared basis of opinion.

To sum up: Soul has arisen at this point because of the Negro's increasingly ambivalent conceptions about the opportunity structure. Earlier, lack of achievement according to American mainstream ideals could easily be explained in terms of impermeable social barriers. Now the impression is gaining ground that there are ways out of the situation. The young men who come under particularly great strain if such a belief is accepted must either achieve (which many of them are obviously still unable to do); explain that achievement is impossible (which is probably no longer true); or explain that achievement according to mainstream ideals is not necessarily achievement according to their *own* ideals. The emergence of soul goes some way toward meeting the need of stating alternative ideals, and also provides solidarity among those with such a need. And it is advantageous to maintain a diffuse conception of soul, for if an intellectually clear definition were established, soul would probably be both less convincing and less uniting.

The view of soul taken here is, in short, one of a piecemeal rhetorical attempt to establish a satisfactory self-image. I am sure that, for the great majority of soul brothers, this is the major basis of soul. It may be added that LeRoi Jones and Charles Keil take a more social-activist view of soul, although Keil tends to make it a prophecy rather than an interpretation. At present, I think that there is little basis for their connecting the majority of soul brothers with militant black nationalism. But organized black nationalism may be able to recruit followers by using some kind of transformed soul vocabulary, and I think there are obviously political attempts now under way to make more of soul. Thus, if at present it is not possible to speak of more than a "rhetoric of soul," it may well be that in the future we will have a "soul movement."

July/August 1968